Praise for
Hero

"Will the real men please stand up? These two brothers of mine, father and son, are standing up in purity, courage, and God-honoring strength. I am proud to know them! Read their story and be encouraged by encountering these modern-day heroes."

—REBECCA ST. JAMES, singer, songwriter, musician

"This story is real. Fred and Jasen are indeed heroes in our time. And through God's grace, you can be too!"

—DR. GARY ROSBERG, founder and CEO, America's Family Coaches, author of *Secrets to a Lasting Love,* and co-founder with wife, Barb, of TheGreatMarriageExperience.com

"*Hero* is my favorite of Fred's books by far. Its keen biblical insights and practical applications are exactly what we need today. I can't stop going through it again and again! I have read many books on dating, but *Hero* easily tops them all. I urge you to read *Hero. This book is that good.* Fred and Jasen, thanks for being the kind of men many of us want to be."

—HEATH ADAMSON, youth evangelist, The Seven Project

"*Hero* is not just another book about dating or purity. As I finished *Hero,* I came to the realization that this book is truly a message from God's heart to ours. I couldn't put it down. I was deeply challenged and inspired by Jasen's words, but most of all, I felt hopeful. As you read this book, I know you'll be changed forever."

—MICHAEL O'BRIEN, former lead singer of Newsong

"God has sounded the battle cry for the hearts of men. Do you hear it? Will you experience the powerful thrill of what it means to be a real man? She needs a hero. Let Fred and Jasen challenge you to become the hero she needs you to be."

—MATT MARKINS, director of the D6 Conference

HERO

Becoming the Man She Desires

FRED STOEKER

Best-selling author of *Every Man's Battle*

& JASEN STOEKER

WITH MIKE YORKEY

WaterBrook
PRESS

HERO

PUBLISHED BY WATERBROOK PRESS
12265 Oracle Boulevard, Suite 200
Colorado Springs, Colorado 80921

All Scripture quotations, unless otherwise indicated, are taken from the Holy Bible, New International Version®. NIV®. Copyright © 1973, 1978, 1984 by International Bible Society. Used by permission of Zondervan Publishing House. All rights reserved. Scripture quotations marked (MSG) are taken from The Message by Eugene H. Peterson. Copyright © 1993, 1994, 1995, 1996, 2000, 2001, 2002. Used by permission of NavPress Publishing Group. All rights reserved. Scripture quotations marked (ESV) are taken from The Holy Bible, English Standard Version, copyright © 2001 by Crossway Bibles, a division of Good News Publishers. Used by permission. All rights reserved.

Italics in Scripture quotations reflect the author's added emphasis.

Details in some anecdotes and stories have been changed to protect the identities of the persons involved.

ISBN 978-1-4000-7109-8
ISBN 978-0-30745-815-5 (electronic)

Published in the United States by WaterBrook Multnomah, an imprint of The Doubleday Publishing Group, a division of Random House Inc., New York.

WATERBROOK and its deer colophon are registered trademarks of Random House Inc.

Library of Congress Cataloging-in-Publication Data
Stoeker, Fred.
    Hero : becoming the man she desires / Fred Stoeker, Jasen Stoeker ; with Mike Yorkey.— 1st ed.
       p. cm.
     ISBN 978-1-4000-7109-8
     1. Men (Christian theology) 2. Sex role — Religious aspects — Christianity. I. Stoeker, Jasen.
II. Yorkey, Mike. III. Title.
     BT703.5.S76 2009
     248.8'42 — dc22

                                    2008044725

Printed in the United States of America
2009 — First Edition

10 9 8 7 6 5 4 3 2 1

SPECIAL SALES

Most WaterBrook Multnomah books are available at special quantity discounts when purchased in bulk by corporations, organizations, and special-interest groups. Custom imprinting or excerpting can also be done to fit special needs. For information, please e-mail SpecialMarkets@WaterBrookMultnomah .com or call 1-800-603-7051.

From Fred:

To Michael
Thanks for stepping into your destiny, Son.
All men know a real man when they see one.
You are one, and there's no doubt about it.

To the Lord
It's true.
You do far more for us than we can ask or even imagine in our wildest dreams.
There is no one like You, and there are no works like Your works.

From Jasen:

To my cheerful, spunky wife, Rose
Without you, I would still be single, and quite unqualified to write this book.
And to our newest little Stoeker resting inside her, who is even now being formed
by the hand of God.
We can't wait to hold you!

CONTENTS

INTRODUCTION

From Fred:

You may already know my story. At one point, one year after graduating from Stanford University, I was sleeping with three different girls and essentially engaged to marry two of them. Suffice it to say, I wasn't leaving girls better off for having known me.

Although I eventually straightened things out and made some incredibly important changes, my testimony is one of failure and redemption. However, I can honestly say that the first person I've known who *has* left every girl better off for having known him is my oldest son, Jasen. Considering his bloodline, this has been a victory of almost unthinkable proportions—certainly beyond anything I could confidently hope for in my early days of fatherhood. But Jasen *has* been victorious, and that's the primary reason I've asked him to share his story with you in this book.

Given his incredible story, you'd think this would have been a pretty obvious idea for me, but it wasn't. I didn't get the idea to team up with Jasen until after I got a call from the beautiful Glen Eyrie conference center in Colorado Springs, asking me to do five sessions on sexual purity for a father-son weekend.

As I pondered what to share with the men, I suddenly realized it would be great for Jasen to share his story. The sons in the audience would love to hear from him, I mused. After all, he's not much older than most of them, and he just made it through eight years of public high school and a state university—exactly where many of them are currently struggling. Who knows more about the practical matters of true heroic purity in today's culture than him?

Glen Eyrie was game, though their enthusiasm became a little guarded when I told the conference leader on the phone that Jasen had never spoken in public about this before. His first talk was scheduled on the Saturday morning of the conference, and as he stepped up to the podium and looked out over the expectant faces of the fathers and their sons around the room, I honestly had no idea what Jasen was planning to say or how he might do as a speaker.

I needn't have been concerned. He hit one out of the park, sharing gripping, courageous accounts from his own battle for purity that even I'd never heard before—stories that left me as awed and speechless as the other guys in the room.

I was an involved father who knew his son well, but even I had no idea what God had in store for all of us through Jasen's words that morning. Sure, I knew what I had taught him along the way, and I know those things gave him a leg up in the battle. But as he spoke on that brisk morning in the shadow of the majestic Pikes Peak, it became abundantly clear to me that Jasen had developed his *own* burning passion for purity, a passion so real and affecting that it hatched its own personal bevy of tools and creative tactics to keep him winning in his battle for purity—things he hadn't learned from me! I'd had no idea just how heroic he had been along the way in school, and as I sat there transfixed, listening to him nail his message home, I shook my head and thought, *What a hero. What a man!*

That morning I became convinced that Jasen, then twenty-three years old and in his first year of marriage, would be the perfect one to join me in writing *Hero,* the book that would complete my trilogy for single guys. *Every Man's Battle* told my story. *Hero* tells "the rest of the story," through Jasen. Here's how I first introduced Jasen to my readers in *Every Man's Battle:*

> My sixteen-year-old son, Jasen, is now a handsome, strapping, six-foot
> adolescent with an easy smile and friendly ways. Not long ago Jasen was
> with friends who had some pornography. He walked away. My son walked
> away. You don't understand what that means to me![1]

As I wrote that paragraph about a decade ago, I dreamed that God would one day break through the generational sin rooted in my family tree, though I had no idea whether that dream would finally come true or fizzle out miserably. Some readers, having briefly "met" Jasen through the pages of *Every Man's Battle,* have written me to ask, "Hey, whatever happened with Jasen? How did his battle turn out?"

Well, if you like happy endings, Jasen's story delivers one for the ages. But if you're looking for a surprise ending, you're out of luck. Our great Father has been the ultimate promise keeper from age to age—He is the same yesterday, today, and forever. How surprised can we be when blessing follows obedience? Jasen's life and marriage are a testament to God's faithfulness for every man out there who still wonders whether heroic purity is really possible in today's culture.

In the following pages, you'll learn some practical ideas from Jasen on how you can walk purely with the women God brings into your life. But what excites me most about *Hero* is what his testimony can do to strengthen your faith. "Worship God! For the testimony of Jesus is the spirit of prophecy" (Revelation 19:10).

The original word for *testimony* can be translated "to do again." And that's where its power lies. When you hear or read a testimony, an atmosphere of faith is created in your heart, and hope swirls through your soul: *If God can do that for him, then He can do it again for me.* That simple faith is all the Holy Spirit needs to duplicate that story in your life and work a major victory once more.

In the end, that's why I believe *Hero* is the ultimate book for single guys. *Every Young Man's Battle* was my first book written to single men, confronting male sexuality within the context of you and your sexual vulnerabilities. It centered on Ephesians 5:3, "But among you there must not be even a hint of sexual immorality." God calls all of us to shut down the sexual gratification we draw through our eyes and minds by "bouncing" our eyes and taking every lustful thought captive.

Tactics, the second book, confronted sexuality within the context of your relationship with God and with your Christian brothers. It challenged you to deepen your intimacy with God and carry your brothers' moral burdens by heeding Jesus's indelible words from the book of Matthew:

"Teacher, which is the greatest commandment in the Law?" Jesus replied:
"'Love the Lord your God with all your heart and with all your soul and

with all your mind.' This is the first and greatest commandment. And the second is like it: 'Love your neighbor as yourself.' All the Law and the Prophets hang on these two commandments." (22:36–40)

Finding intimacy with God and with your neighbor changes every man's battle forever, primarily by replacing your hunger for the false intimacy of porn and masturbation with the genuine intimacy of true relationship with God and genuine connection with the men around you.

In *Hero,* the context is your relationship with women. Our guiding verse this time is "Treat…younger women as sisters, with absolute purity" (1 Timothy 5:1–2).

In this third book, the battle for purity comes full circle. Expanding on the theme from the final chapters of *Every Young Man's Battle,* we focus on this central question: are you leaving the women in your life better off for having known you? It's a vital question. That's precisely God's challenge to *every* man of any age. And it applies to all single men, whether you're seventeen or seventy.

Leaving her better off for having known you is a heroic, even chivalrous goal. Yet the truth is, when it comes to women, most of us think very little about our level of heroism when dating. As guys, we tend to think first about how we can come across as the coolest guy on the planet, closely followed by how well we're honing that public perception of perfection: *What should I wear? How should I act? What should I say?*

Trouble is, while being cool may catch a girl's eye, it's not the greatest strategy for winning her heart. This mind-set does little to keep you sexually pure during the relationship and ultimately only makes matters more difficult. In light of that, be honest with yourself for a moment. When it comes to your sexual purity, how has your quest for cool been working out for you in your dating relationships?

If the results have been less than stellar, don't despair. I believe you can be both cool and heroic when it comes to your most significant relationships. But being godly and heroic must take precedence over being cool if you expect to stay pure while dating. And to help you see how that looks in practice, I'll be offering my firstborn son, Jasen, as Exhibit A. You'll hear a lot more about Jasen and *from* Jasen in the coming pages.

As you read his testimony, we sincerely hope that a deep faith will arise in your soul, a belief that God will "do it again" in your life. We hope the Lord will turn your heart further toward Jesus in your approach to dating, and if you'll honor us a moment, we'd like to offer a prayer of dedication toward that end, here at the start of your journey through these pages:

> *God, we come to You in Jesus's name, thanking You for these moments with our brother who now holds this book in his hands. We know You are hungry to speak to Your sons about their relationships, and at this particular moment, You are especially hungry to reach out to touch this brother's heart with Your great love. Capture him. Make Your intense desires his. Call him away from the darker desires that lurk around us all, and call out the heroic heart You've placed within him. As he stands up for You in his relationships, multiply the impact of his obedience across our nation and around our world. We ask a lot, Lord, because we know You yearn to do it. Encourage this man to seek You earnestly, Lord. Open his ears and his eyes, that He might find You.*

1

VICTORY

From Fred:

The crowd's roar shocked me. It was similar to the shouts of triumph I'd heard many times at football games, after a last-second Hail Mary pass into the end zone, or an interception that propels the home team into the play-offs. I've heard it at baseball games, when the walk-off blast disappears into a whooping, surging sea of delirium in the left-field bleachers.

But I'd never heard such raucous cheers at a wedding.

The formal ceremony had been rapidly moving toward a close when a smiling Pastor Dave Olson cheerfully proclaimed, "Jasen, you may kiss your bride!"

And that's when it happened. As my son happily wrapped his newly minted wife in his arms and their lips met for the first time, a spontaneous, ear-bursting roar grew into a frenzy as our exuberant guests leapt to their feet. They whooped and hollered as if they were witnessing a March Madness buzzer-beater, crowing and hugging and pumping their fists, their boisterous shouts and piercing whistles of jubilation ricocheting from the rafters.

I stood there dumbfounded, a bobble-headed Fred doll with a silly grin plastered across my speechless face. My head bounced crazily about as I grappled to absorb everything at once in this confounding scene. I'd expected my emotions to swell in a flash flood of joyful tears at this point in the ceremony. But instead, I stood transfixed, motionless, mesmerized by the moment, frozen by a deep, still awe for the handsome young groom beaming radiantly into the luminous eyes of his lovely bride.

Who was this guy? And why were they cheering him like Tiger Woods at the final hole of a major? This was my son, my firstborn, the culmination of my efforts, the one whose spiritual destiny had turned and twisted and joined with mine from our earliest days together.

During the final days leading up to his wedding, I was like any groom's father, I suppose. My mind couldn't help replaying the great and poignant moments of our lives together. I was wildly emotional, especially as I recalled his toddler days when his shiny, loving eyes challenged me to the core and altered the destiny of our family tree.

Such a cute little squirt, he was one great big ball of herky-jerky, drooling action. At times he'd amble awkwardly over to me with a drippy pacifier stuck loosely in his mouth, holding it in somehow while shooting me a goofy grin as big as the moon. Though he couldn't speak, I knew exactly what his eyes were saying, as clear as a bell: *Daddy, you are my hero. I want to grow up to be just like you!*

Many times I'd simply sweep him into my arms and tickle him, I loved him so much. But other times, when we were home alone together, I'd burst into hopeless tears.

No! I'd beg inside. *Please don't become like me, Son!*

You see, I was no hero. The truth of my family's generational curse was all too familiar to me. My sexual sin would one day doom him to the same cold, heartless jail cell that sucked the life from my soul, the very same prison in which my dad and grandfathers writhed until death freed them from the icy chains. *I'm not your hero, Son. If I was, I could save you from this prison. But I can't even save myself! How will I ever save you?*

Sometimes, I'd lie awake wide-eyed near dawn, staring at the ceiling as silent screams pierced my soul. *God, how can You be so cruel? Why did You give me a son? I'm not fit to raise him, and You know it! You've given me the spiritual responsibility for him, but I don't have what it takes to do the job. What were You thinking?*

He was likely thinking that He'd help me rise up to the challenge somehow, but I just couldn't envision Him pulling off *that* one, despite His omnipotence. Undeterred, the Lord somehow used a simple sermon one Sunday morning to launch a sizzling cascade of truth on me that changed the course of my life—and Jasen's—forever.

I can remember the verses as if I'd just read them this morning:

> This is the word that came to Jeremiah from the LORD… "Go to the Recabite family and invite them to come to one of the side rooms of the house of the LORD and give them wine to drink."… Then I set bowls full of wine and some cups before the men of the Recabite family and said to them, "Drink some wine." But they replied, "We do not drink wine, because our forefather Jonadab son of Recab gave us this command: 'Neither you nor your descendants must ever drink wine….' We have obeyed everything our forefather Jonadab son of Recab commanded us. Neither we nor our wives nor our sons and daughters have ever drunk wine." (Jeremiah 35:1–2, 5–6, 8)

Obedient children impress God, and He was so pleased with Jonadab's offspring that He used them as an example to His own people:

> This is what the LORD Almighty, the God of Israel, says: Go and tell the men of Judah and the people of Jerusalem, "Will you not learn a lesson and obey my words?" declares the LORD. "Jonadab son of Recab ordered his sons not to drink wine and this command has been kept. To this day they do not drink wine, because they obey their forefather's command. But I have spoken to you again and again, yet you have not obeyed me." (Jeremiah 35:13–14)

These are stern words, and worthy of our attention on any day. But these weren't the words that pummeled my soul that morning. No, I was hammered by a little-known fact about this passage, shared by my pastor from the pulpit. Do you know how much time had passed between the days of Jonadab and this day, when Jeremiah asked Jonadab's "sons" to drink wine with him? As many as three hundred years! Jonadab was such a great example of godliness that his descendants were still following his example three centuries later.

My soul ignited. *Can this work for my sexual sin? If I can manage to win this battle and teach my children to follow me this way, will my descendants still be saying three hundred years from now, "We don't look at pornography because our father Fred didn't look at porn"?*

My Deepest Fear

God's truth had seized my heart, and I began to wrestle with the possibilities. You can read the full story in my book *Tactics*, but all the grappling hinged on one uncertainty: even if I did manage to win the battle myself, how could I be sure that Jasen would follow? I couldn't change the destiny of my family tree by myself. Someone would have to step up to the challenge with me.

Who must that someone be? Answer: that stubby-legged, drooling little kid who thought I was his hero. That was my deepest fear. How could I reach him or any other son I might have? I had no idea what kind of man he would become, and I wasn't too sure I was willing to risk all the effort to change my family tree with that kind of uncertainty hanging over me. I waffled seriously over this issue for months until my exasperated Father in heaven spoke this chilling challenge into my heart one morning: *Are you going to drive the stake into the ground right here and change the destiny of your family tree, or will you be leaving the job for some man better than you, somewhere down the line?*

The exchange broke me into tears. I couldn't stand the kind of man I was, the kind that the Lord couldn't trust on the big things. I'd spent my whole life in sports and school trying to prove that I had what it takes to be a man, a guy you could count on in the clutch. Would I really slink back now, when it really mattered? Was I really going to let another male offspring "down the line" finish the job for me, some man who loved Him more, someone more committed to

His purposes than I was? My heart writhed in grinding torment. It was *my* family tree and *my* battle to fight. What kind of tepid, fainthearted man depends on someone else to restore his family name?

Worst of all, if I passed on this, I knew the Lord would one day lay that same challenge at Jasen's feet. Would my son become that man who was better than me? I didn't know the answer, but I wasn't about to leave such a brutal battle up to my precious son to fight alone. That sealed the deal for me, because that just wasn't going to happen. No matter how miserably I might fail in the battle, he was my boy, and he wouldn't have to battle this horrid thing by himself.

I knew this was the defining moment of my life. I could either "man up" and pick a fight with this brutal taskmaster, or I could drift meekly into the same retreating rabble of Stoeker men and spend the rest of my days merely posing as a man, as they had.

As a student of history, I already knew how real men thought in the face of battle. Teddy Roosevelt said sternly, "No man is worth calling a man who will not fight rather than submit to infamy or see those that are dear to him suffer wrong." Winston Churchill declared resolutely, "What is the use of living, if it be not to strive for noble causes and to make this muddled world a better place for those who will live in it after we are gone?"

Was I worth calling a "man"? And if not, what was the use of living?

The time for posing and hiding was over. If I didn't step up and fight right now, I *knew* I would someday toss on my bed and fight off the desperate, hopeless regrets night after night, like so many other timid souls who flee from battle in this world. In the end, I couldn't stand that thought. I was desperate enough as it was, but at least there was still hope! I wanted freedom from sexual sin, and it was time to face up to the raging war at hand. My family's destiny depended upon it and, I knew, my own manhood as well.

I finally engaged the battle for keeps just a few days later. Driving on Merle Hay Road near my house, I found myself lusting once more at a jogger, and I broke down one more time. Pounding my fists on the steering wheel, I shouted through my tears, "It stops here! I'm not going to live like this anymore! I don't know how to build a covenant with my eyes, but I'm going to learn! It stops here!" Within six weeks of fighting, the tide of battle turned decidedly in my favor, and by the end of three years, every rebellious skirmish had been put down. Against all odds, I stood victorious over my enemy in this ruthless fight, completing my part of the bargain. I'd driven that stake deeply into the ground.

But now it was Jasen's turn. How would he respond?

My first clue came when he turned eleven. We'd spent many treasured evenings together reading Dr. James Dobson's classic *Preparing for Adolescence*. When we came to the section on pornography, I told him, "Jace, looking at pornography is like taking drugs. When we look at women without their clothes on, there is a chemical reaction that happens in our brain that is much like the reaction the brain has to taking cocaine…the studies were even showing this way back when I was at Stanford. I watched some of my rich dorm friends blow thousands and thousands of dollars on cocaine in just a few days over spring break…they just couldn't get enough."

I let that thought settle in before continuing. "Jasen, I've never done cocaine, but I *have* viewed pornography, and once I did, I was hooked and wanted to see more and more, just like those guys with their drugs. It was a brutal habit to break, and I just don't want you to make the same mistake I did."

Wouldn't you know it? Two weeks later, Jasen's classmates brought some pornography to school—a *Hustler* magazine. They called him over to peek at the glossy pages.

That night, when Jasen shared this amazing story with me, I was frozen by his words. *Oh, no! This is it! His battle has begun. What did he do?* As a Stoeker, my past should have been his prologue: getting hooked by porn at a young age, then getting caught up in premarital sex during high school and college, and perhaps later, if he was like his grandfather or great-grandfather, ditching his wife after committing numerous sexual affairs. He would be the fourth-generation Stoeker following in the family footsteps. Struggling to control my breath, I asked, "Son, what did you do?"

"I walked away, Dad, just like you said I should."

I swallowed back the lump in my throat and sucked in a huge breath, grabbing him and hugging him before he ran off to his room. My heart soared. *God!* I thought. *You're doing it! My son walked away!* Right there on the kitchen tile, I danced a little jig. *Could this be the first crack in the generational curse?* I could barely allow myself to hope, but I was gripped by the incredible thought, *He could actually win this thing, God.* God was clearly up to the challenge, and obviously, Jasen was too. Even at eleven, he heard my "Don't do as I did" counsel and wasn't afraid to walk away from the crowd when offered an easy opportunity to sin.

My son was a stud.

Victory March

That incident in the schoolyard turned out to be the first of hundreds of cracks that Jasen would hammer into the curse during his teens and early twenties. By the grace of God and by the promises He offers us all, that massive wall of corruption now sits in a pile of dusty rubble.

Jasen stood atop that debris at his wedding, utterly victorious, and that's why a common, ordinary church wedding turned into a thunderous parade of triumph.

As Jasen's celebratory march into matrimony passed before me that afternoon, my pride swelled and my mind raced wildly. As his comrade in that battle for our family destiny, let me offer some inside color commentary and a few action highlights from the wedding that day, which opened this way:

> On behalf of the Gibson and Stoeker families, it is an honor to welcome you
> to share this joyous occasion and to witness the vows of this precious couple.

The first thought that had me sitting there marveling was, *I can't believe this! Jasen actually got a girl!* That may sound strange from his father, but as college graduation inched ever closer and Jasen still hadn't ever found a serious girlfriend, my heart moaned for him. I wondered if I'd been wrong to encourage such a strong stand against impurity. *So few women are living this way!* I thought. *Have I doomed him to decades of loneliness?*

I'd always trusted God to take care of him, and I'd always told Jasen that God was completely trustworthy to find a mate for the man who takes Him at His Word when it comes to his purity. "God's blessing for you is sure, Son," I promised. "God isn't God if He doesn't keep His Word."

And he believed me! His faith rarely wavered over finding such a woman who would willingly stand with him in purity. Sadly, behind the scenes my own confidence flagged miserably at times, and the same was true with my wife, Brenda. After all, his unrelenting, determined stand for purity ran counter to the widespread sensuality in the girls his age, even among those from Christian high schools and colleges.

At times, I despaired. *Are there any women left out there who care enough about their purity that they could live with Jasen's and God's standards? And even if there is one out there, how will Jasen ever find her?* As graduation loomed ever larger on the horizon, my hope was fizzling. I'd have been grateful for any mousy, leftover girl God might toss his way.

But not Jasen. And now as I looked up at my son standing so proudly at the altar while awaiting his bride, my thoughts turned to that impossibly perfect girl standing just outside the sanctuary, draped in satin and lace. Inside, I laughed at myself. *What a dork you were, Fred! You despaired too soon, buddy!* It turns out God *is* exactly as I'd tried to tell Jasen—faithful to the end. And even though I had some trouble fully believing it at times, all my preaching about His goodness had been spot on. God didn't mess around when it came to His boy Jasen. He didn't have just any girl for him.

Let me tell you about the girl who entered the crowded hall that afternoon. Rose Gibson was a stunning catch, vivaciously bubbly, incredibly beautiful, and so alive in Christ. She was not only a high school homecoming queen but the pinnacle of a perfect match for Jasen. I never thought I'd ever meet another woman like the one I'd married, yet there she stood, about to marry my son.

As Rose stepped and paused, stepped and paused her way down the center aisle, her regal manner overwhelmed me. This wasn't just another lovely bride walking up one more aisle. This was the unmatched, incandescent favor of the living God slipping by us, fittingly clothed in brilliant white.

"Who gives this woman to be married to this man?"

As David Gibson lifted his daughter's veil to kiss her goodbye, his countenance sparkled with pride and joy over his one and only precious daughter, just as mine did with Jasen. I glanced back at Jace, and I couldn't help thinking about the dad who *wasn't* there that day, my father who'd died seven years earlier. How would *he* have felt about this couple?

He'd have thought you were chumps, I thought.

Fred Stoeker Sr. was a great man. He was a *man's* man. An AAU heavyweight national champion wrestler, he could drain his opponent's will to win in mere moments. At the poker table, he could drain your wallet just as fast. He could out-fish, out-work, and out-charm nearly any man on earth—and he had a string of mistresses to prove it. In fact, nothing and no one that I know of ever got the best of my dad. Except for one thing.

Sex.

When it came to sex, there was only one truth for Dad: real men know women as early and as often as they can. It didn't matter whether you were married, or whether you claimed Christ. Dad knew the "real" truth about manhood, and he wasn't about to let the Bible or anything else get in the way.

Fred Sr. paved his own path regardless of the consequences, and he raced with his truth all the way to his finish line. Just before his death, when it was finally apparent that even he couldn't out-bluff Father Time, he told me that divorcing my mom (because of his skirt chasing) was the dumbest decision he'd ever made in his life. "Your mom was a good woman, and I threw her away," he admitted in a moment of candor. "And do you know what? I never recovered from that mistake, no matter how hard I tried. I never recovered financially, no matter how hard I worked. I never had another relationship any better than the one I had with your mom, though I've known many women. And worst of all, I've never been able to really rebuild my relationships with you kids like I wanted to because of the pain of that divorce."

When I asked why he chose to chase those other women, he said it just seemed like the thing to do in those days. It was the sixties, when sexual liberation was the war cry on college campuses and the nightly news. "It was the early days of the Playboy generation. Having a mistress was something men did to prove they were sophisticated, you know? To show they were with it, with the times. I never really thought it through, though, Son. That's really all it was."

So even though he'd never really thought his philosophies through and even though his "truth" had ruined relationship after relationship with women over the years, he somehow managed to remain certain it was always best to take your girlfriends to bed, especially if the relationship looked like things were heading for the altar. According to him, you needed to know if you were "sexually compatible" with your woman before you tied the knot. That is why he pulled me aside right after I'd announced my engagement to Brenda and shared this pocketful of advice: "Son, I know what the Bible says about premarital sex, and you and I are both Christians and everything. But sex is too important for you to get married without having intercourse with Brenda first. You can't afford to marry a frigid girl."

Dad was a great role model in many ways, but in the arena of sex, he was a disaster. And as I gazed up at Jasen on his great day of triumph, I was amused to think that if my father were still alive, the guy who had *never* owned his sexuality for a moment would be scoffing at his grandson who had *always* owned his.

I glanced over at my younger son, Michael, standing next to Jasen as his best man. Just a year earlier, in his last year of middle school, Michael had already been jeered by his junior high classmates for avoiding PG-13 movies and derided by his teammates in the locker room for choosing to put off dating indefinitely. Michael owned his sexuality, yet he was being mocked by these middle-school guys who didn't own theirs, just like my father might have mocked Jasen that day at the wedding.

Suddenly, it hit me. I realized that for all of my father's greatness in sports and business, he had never matured past these middle schoolers in regard to his sexuality, even knocking me, his own son, for waiting on sex until marriage. *Weird,* I thought. *I wonder how many men get stuck in a junior-high mentality when it comes to sex?*

I returned my focus to Pastor Dave, who was preaching wonderfully on God's plan for marriage and expertly dissecting scriptural meaning behind the covenants involved. And then, all too soon my reverie was broken and those very vows were upon us, ready to be made. Jasen made his vows, and then Rose. "With this ring, I give myself to you, Jasen, to be your faithful wife. All that I have is yours. From this day forward, I will support you, as you lead our family to follow Christ."

Just then, I was struck by another thought. *God's presence has been unbelievable during this ceremony.* At first, I'd passed it off as parental pride skewing my perception. But as the proceedings continued, His powerful, holy presence in that sanctuary had grown unmistakable as Jasen and Rose exchanged their vows. Later at the reception, literally *dozens* of our friends and acquaintances mentioned that they had felt God's presence in that hall.

I've never experienced a more powerful wedding ceremony. The Holy Spirit was clearly overjoyed with this young couple and their commitment to sexual purity, and as the ceremony neared its close, Pastor Dave shared his final words. I believe they explain why the Lord allowed His presence to be felt so deeply by so many of us that afternoon:

Well, this is that special moment—the kiss—that we all look forward to at the end of every wedding. But before we do this, let me share something with you. This is certainly the moment we're always waiting for, but it's especially true in regards to this couple. Many of you may not realize that Jasen and Rose really have waited until marriage, and this is going to be their very first kiss. Some of you may already be aware of that, and you may feel it is a little silly and old-fashioned. But I think it's a beautiful thing, and I really believe that this is the way God intended it.

We just talked about what a covenant relationship means before God, but now let's take a look at how the Lord's temple completes the picture of marital covenant for us. In the temple, there was a veil at the entrance to the Holy of Holies. In order to go beyond that veil and to worship the Lord, the high priest had to first enter into blood covenant with Him. What's interesting is that in the original language of Scripture, the word used for worship was *proskuneo*, or "kiss." In other words, only the man in covenant with God could pass beyond the temple's veil and "kiss" the Lord in worship.

"This couple's relationship has followed that same pattern as they've approached their marital covenant, and I think the Lord is very pleased with that. When it comes to relationships between men and women, God is clear that a man must be in covenant with a woman before he goes in to her. As a man, Jasen has willingly waited until this moment, the moment he's entered into covenant with Rose. He has accepted the position of high priest for her, and he has accepted the responsibility of representing her before the throne of God as leader of his family.

Now that he has done so, his wait is finally over, and that special moment has arrived. Since Jasen has just entered into covenant with Rose, he can now go beyond the veil—her wedding veil—and kiss his bride.

So now, it is with especially great pleasure that, in the power vested in me by Jesus Christ, His Church, and the state of Iowa, I now pronounce you man and wife. Jasen, you may kiss your bride.

And then the great roar arose, surprising me and mesmerizing me at once. What was I feeling? Simple. Absolute, unadulterated awe for my son. Jasen had run his race. He had finished the course. From those unsettling earliest days of puberty to this grand, exultant moment at the altar, Jasen had never touched a woman's body in dishonor. Rose was the first girl he'd ever kissed, the first girl he'd ever seriously dated. He'd never left a girl worse off for having known him. He'd owned his sexuality completely.

And my first and only thought at that moment was the one spoken silently in my heart, over and over again throughout the day. *You're a greater man than I ever dreamed of being, Jace. You are the greatest man I know.*

I meant those words with every fiber of my being, and I still mean them today.

Still, it does seem kind of funny if you stop to think about it. After all, all Jasen did was obey God's call to every man. Why is his story so remarkable?

The answer is: because of what surrounds him—and you—every day. The sickness seething into every crevice of society—this evil virus bent on getting you to bow down before its unholy god, our great American idol—

Baal.

2

BAAL

Why do guys like Jasen come along so rarely? The answer has much to do with what we're sowing and reaping as a nation. The sexual climate wasn't always this hot in America, but then again, we only started "sowing the wind" about fifty years ago: "They sow the wind and reap the whirlwind. The stalk has no head; it will produce no flour. Were it to yield grain, foreigners would swallow it up" (Hosea 8:7). We're reaping the whirlwind, all right. And we're seeing things today many of us thought we'd never see, even in churches.

Pastors used to advise us to keep our heads down whenever Hollywood opened fire on our sexuality. Today, way too many insecure, seeker-friendly youth pastors are leveling us with friendly fire in their sincere desire to be "relevant." Although our male hard-wiring is prone to addictive lusts of the eyes, young Christian leaders often approve and even promote sensual movies that rev up guys' sexual engines into the red zone. Some even share entertaining film clips during their services that would have made their grandparents blush and then throw kerosene on the fire by screening full-length R-rated and PG-13 movies in their small group get-togethers, in spite of the nudity and the embarrassing amounts of sexual innuendo. When asked how they justify showing such films to those they're mentoring, they shrug carelessly, "They're watching these movies anyway. Why not use them to connect with the guys?"

Why not, indeed? No wonder the students on our Christian campuses are as hooked on sensuality as the ones attending secular universities like Iowa State, where Jasen went to school. When my daughter was checking out colleges, we visited a well-respected Christian campus in the Chicago area, and our tour host pulled me aside. "Last year we put in campus-wide Internet. The day it went live, it crashed."

"What was the problem?"

"Porn sites," she said. "We had so many guys rushing to look at porn that we had to completely shut it down after just a few hours."

Shortly after, I was asked to speak at another respected Christian college. Prior to my visit, students were anonymously surveyed about their use of porn. I was only mildly surprised to find that every male student admitted to viewing cyber porn *every week*. But the real shocker was this: 87 percent of the girls were doing the same thing.

That's a quick snapshot of the moral free-fall of our Christian culture in the past five decades. Our broader secular culture has fared no better. In the *Father Knows Best* era of the 1950s, no self-respecting girl would ever have been seen in public with too little on, and her dad would have said something about it before she left the house. Now she's embarrassed to be seen with too *much* on—even in church. Somehow, girls got the idea they wouldn't be attractive or be able to attract guys without putting everything on display.

How did this happen, you ask?

It looks like Baal is making a major-league comeback.

Baal is the pagan god of fertility, one of the chief false gods of the Canaanites in the Old Testament. The customs associated with Baal worship included fertility rituals that elevated sex to a sacred pursuit, which eventually led the Israelites into sin and ultimately resulted in their destruction.

Baal worship is a pernicious form of paganism that views the world as feminine, our "Mother Earth." Baal was the male sun god who would rain down his seed to impregnate Mother Earth so that she could "deliver" the fruit of her "womb" in the form of crops, thereby sustaining her "children." In these ancient agricultural societies, survival depended on appeasing the sun god Baal in order to receive his rain from the skies.

Behind every religious cult, of course, is a spirit bent on turning men away from the true God through false practices of worship. What did this spirit of Baal demand as worship? Sex. How convenient to have divine approval of our lusts! The followers of Baal built an entire cult system to worship him through culturally sanctioned orgies, using temple prostitutes and public displays of virility at his altar.

We know from the Old Testament that there were times when the men of Israel bowed before the god of Baal, accepting that blank check to indulge in sexual immorality with the loose women hanging around the altars. That sounds fairly primitive to us these days, and it's no surprise that God was not amused by their actions.

But while we may seem far more sophisticated in *our* eyes, we really aren't all that far off from those guys in God's eyes, and as we bow before the spirit of Baal in our dating relationships, He's no more amused by us now than He was by them. After all, He never forgets what we often do: when we go too far with girls outside of marriage, we're actually practicing a form of idolatry.

That's right. Sex outside marriage is *idolatry*. Most of us believe we're far more sophisticated than our ignorant ancestors, so we pass it off, sniffing and saying, "Come on, we don't have *idols* anymore!" We laugh at the mental images of naked heathens leaping over flames and writhing to pounding drums, one arm slinging about a splashing jug of wine and the other squeezing a laughing, voluptuous woman.

But come on. As Christians, we ought to know better than that. Our apostle Paul made no distinction between sexual immorality and idolatry:

> But among you there must not be even a hint of sexual immorality, or of
> any kind of impurity, or of greed, because these are improper for God's
> holy people. Nor should there be obscenity, foolish talk or coarse joking,
> which are out of place, but rather thanksgiving. For of this you can be sure:
> No immoral, impure or greedy person—*such a man is an idolater*—has
> any inheritance in the kingdom of Christ and of God. (Ephesians 5:3–5)

Paul was inspired elsewhere to instruct us that we shouldn't be ignorant of the devil's strategies. Perhaps it's time we learn how the old spirit of Baal is still tripping people up today. In spite of our enlightened intellects and sophistication, what I'm about to share will show you just how similar our cultural free-fall has been to the Israelites'—and exactly why heroes like Jasen are on the verge of extinction.

BACK TO THE FUTURE

The story begins during the great exodus, when Moses led 600,000 men of Israel toward the Promised Land a few millennia ago. As they set up camp along the Jordan River on the plains of Moab, the king, called Balak, became terrified. He'd been watching Israel's multitudes march past his threatened kingdom, and he knew he could never defeat such a vast army. So Balak invested a good sum of money with five elders of Moab and Midian to hire a famous diviner and sorcerer named Balaam to curse the Israelites.

However, God had already told Balaam that he must never place a curse on Israel, because they were blessed of the Lord. So Balaam refused to come back with the king's men. Undeterred, King Balak sent an even larger contingent of distinguished leaders with an even more handsome reward. When Balaam prayed about it, God consented to allow him to go, but only under strict orders: "Go with these men, but do only what I tell you to do and speak only what I tell you to speak."

When King Balak heard that Balaam was coming, he rushed out to meet him at the border of his domain, and at sunrise the next morning, King Balak escorted Balaam to a high place overlooking the plains of Moab—a place where they could look out and see a portion of the people of Israel. After building seven altars and sacrificing seven bulls and rams, Balaam went off to a barren height to meet with the Lord.

Afterward, Balaam returned to the altar where the king and all the princes of Moab were waiting for him to speak this first oracle:

Balak brought me from Aram, the king of Moab from the eastern mountains. "Come," he said, "curse Jacob for me; come, denounce Israel." How can I curse those whom God has not cursed? How can I denounce those whom the LORD has not denounced? From the rocky peaks I see them, from the heights I view them. I see a people who live apart and do not consider themselves one of the nations. Who can count the dust of Jacob or number the fourth part of Israel? Let me die the death of the righteous, and may my end be like theirs! (Numbers 23:7–10)

When King Balak heard this oration of blessing over the people of Israel, he was spitting mad! "What have you done to me? I brought you to curse my enemies, but you have done nothing but bless them!" (Numbers 23:11).

Balaam reminded him that he could only speak what the Lord put in his mouth. The king was frustrated with this sorcerer, but since he was also out of any better options, he took Balaam to another high place, hoping that the Lord would allow him to curse the Israelites from there. Balaam again blessed them. Balak tried a third time, and Balaam blessed them once more. King Balak went ballistic. "Leave at once and go home! I said I would reward you handsomely, but the LORD has kept you from being rewarded" (24:11).

Balaam calmly answered Balak. "I [can't] go beyond the command of the LORD—and I must say only what the LORD says. Now I am going back to my people" (verses 13–14).

Unfortunately, Balaam didn't go straight back to his people. He was going to get that reward one way or another because he was not the man of God he'd been pretending to be. He was a man of greed, and he was soon hatching a new plan to rake in some cash, traitorously betraying God's people behind the scenes just after he finished blessing them from the mountaintop.

Quietly, he pulled King Balak aside and made him an offer he couldn't refuse, telling the king, in so many words, "If you want to take these people out, entice them to start sinning. Once they do, God will take their protection away, and then they can be conquered" (Revelation 2:14; Numbers 31:16).

Intrigued, King Balak followed Balaam's advice and sent a bevy of beautiful Moabite women into Hebrew territory. Their mission: tempt the Israelite men to follow them back to the pagan temples in Moab to gorge themselves on food and sex. But how were God's men swayed so easily to participate in orgy sex on a pagan altar?

Stop for a moment and fix this picture in your mind. The Israelite camp was overflowing with heroic, pure Jewish men and boys living in a chaste culture, their hearts and minds set upon the Lord and His promises to drive out all their enemies as they made their way toward their Promised Land. Suddenly, a handful of Moabite babes slip into camp and tug on their sleeves, coyly winking and purring, "Come with us; we have something special to share with you!"

These God-fearing men of war then made a greenhorn mistake in every man's battle. They didn't bounce their eyes and turn away. Instead, their eyes got wide, their throats went dry, and they were soon skipping back over the plains with the Moabites and bowing to Baal.

Balaam's plan worked. After the Israelites' moral failure, God's anger burned, and 24,000 men died in the resulting plague.

PARALLELS FROM THE PAST

This story strongly parallels what's happening in our country today. Though we aren't literally His "chosen people," our nation was largely settled by God-fearing men and women who voyaged from Europe yearning for a "Promised Land" flowing with spiritual milk and honey, a place founded upon principles of His Word, where godly people could worship the Lord freely, as they saw fit. Family after courageous family boarded creaky ships for a long passage to the New World during the seventeenth and eighteenth centuries, and soon a brave, godly people were blessing God openly throughout the land, kindling His light in their new homes and fanning it brightly before the nations.

God blessed the United States incredibly in return. Not only did He make America that "shining city on a hill" for many oppressed peoples around the world, He also spared this country from much of the destruction, mayhem, and murder that marked most of the twentieth century.

Satan despised and feared America, and he yearned to snuff out that light, just like King Balak yearned to snuff out the Jews. Spewing curses in every direction, he first tried to take us out directly, using a deranged maniac named Adolf Hitler to whip up the winds of war across the nations. The ensuing global conflict took 72 million lives during World War II but left America relatively unscathed. One might argue that God turned Satan's curses into blessings, just as He had with Balaam, and America emerged from World War II stronger than before, the richest nation on the earth.

As Satan brushed away the dust and debris of his defeat, he paused to mull things over. *They are immune to my curses! God's protecting them, and as long as they are walking with Him, He will keep blessing them…until…wait a minute…I know what I can do.*

When I was trying to block those Jews from the Promised Land, God wouldn't let me curse the Jews directly. So I tricked that sorcerer Balaam into telling the king to seduce Israel with easy sex, and those fools fell for it, easy as pie. Maybe it's time to pull out that old play and run it against America. If I can entice them to cross the moral lines and bow before another altar, God will take their protection away, and they'll be mine. But who will be my Balaam this time around?

It turns out that a twenty-seven-year-old Chicago advertising executive named Hugh Hefner was happy to volunteer his services. His first *Playboy* magazine hit newsstands in 1953 featuring Marilyn Monroe on the cover and a naked Marilyn Monroe inside. Marilyn became the first of Hef's "Moabite women" inviting us to a new, sensual form of worship—widespread pornography—that initially shocked us but soon spread quickly through tacit acceptance. A mere fifty years later, our culture has become so sensual that our Moabite women have gone digital, and their pixilated forms slip into our lives any time of day or night on instant demand.

What Hefner and others of his ilk wrought was the mainstreaming of pornography and the decoupling of sex from a committed, marital relationship.

The return of Baal's altar was passed off as "sexual liberation," and American men began rushing through doors that had remained closed for centuries. Soon, a "new spirit" began taking over our lives.

It wasn't really new, of course. This was the spirit of Baal, as ancient as the altars of Moab, with a distinct progression to its pattern of influence that serves as a fingerprint in our land, implicating our culprit. Remember, spirits never die. They just keep seeking one more opportunity to impose their personality and influence upon the lives of individuals, families, and, ultimately, nations.

Just as it was with the Israelites, when Baal's boy Hugh Hefner sent his frolicking waves of curvaceous Moabites into our lives, we didn't engage every man's battle or bounce our eyes away. Instead, our eyes got wide, our throats went dry, and soon we were bowing sexually with these lovely strangers upon our beds in our dorms and homes.

It didn't look like idolatry at first, and before long it didn't look like sin much anymore, either, because everything was glossed over with a veneer of sophistication, which was all by design. Hefner staked out where he wanted to take *Playboy* and its male readers in his first editor's letter. "We enjoy mixing cocktails and an hors d'oeuvre or two," he opined, "putting a little mood music on the phonograph and inviting a female acquaintance for a quiet discussion on Picasso, Nietzsche, sex."[1]

That was the foundation of what became known as the "Playboy philosophy," which was that men did not have to limit their sex drive to their wives but were free to chase after any woman willing to share an evening of sexual delight. It became the popular culture of the day—guys reading *Playboy* and drinking highballs and ignoring their wives and children, while they were out clubbing because it was cool and sophisticated. This was the first distinctive swirl of Baal's fingerprint upon our nation, which is always the first telltale mark of his progression of influence, just as it was in Moab for the Jews: *men begin choosing their lusts over God's purposes for their lives and families.*

From there, cultural changes rolled in like a flood. The April 8, 1966, issue of *Time* magazine posed this provoking question on its cover: "Is God Dead?" The cover story argued that He was. The following year, the "Summer of Love" descended on Haight-Ashbury in San Francisco as 100,000 young people converged to kick off the free-love movement, some of them running naked through the crowds and diving deeply into depravity. After opening the door to "casual sex" en masse, the "Liberated Youth" returned to hometowns as evangelists of their new philosophy.

New books emerged about "open marriages" and "swinging" (the euphemism for spouse-swapping), along with the reminder that America should become "more enlightened sexually." The Hollywood film industry abandoned its self-imposed censorship guidelines in 1968, opening the floodgates to X-rated films like *Midnight Cowboy*, celebrated as the best picture of the year by the Academy of Motion Picture Arts and Sciences in 1970.

In 1973, the Supreme Court legalized abortion-on-demand, an attempt to cut out the consequences of sin. While new to us, this was actually the predictable next step in the pattern of Baal's influence. *Child sacrifice* has always been the second distinctive swirl in Baal's fingerprint, because promiscuous sex leads to babies, a very inconvenient mess indeed.

The temple prostitutes in Baal worship didn't have access to birth control, of course, so there were a lot of unwanted children. Since there were no social nets to protect the mother and child, the temple priests had no alternative but to fashion a new ritual, incinerating babies inside the fiery belly of the idol and celebrating it as an act of adoration to their god.

Our altars of sexual sin also delivered millions of unplanned pregnancies too, so we reestablished the same old ritual, only now marketed under a clever new name. Our "abortions" are performed at "reproductive health clinics" by employing vacuums, chemicals, and extraction devices instead of flames. Just as it was in the days of old, abortion—our child sacrifice—is revered as a sacrament in many feminist circles, an act of adoration to the god of sexual fulfillment.

One generation later, we're reaping the whirlwind as a nation, and our culture is in its twilight. Porn is just another form of protected free speech. The sex drive is seen as equivalent to hunger and thirst, so it must be satiated, inside or outside of marriage. Homosexuality is an "alternative lifestyle" we're forced to endorse. Child porn and pedophilia are epidemic, and girls and boys are being abducted into servitude as child porn stars and sex slaves.

All in the name of doing your own thing.

Buying In

When a *Los Angeles Times* reporter asked Hugh Hefner recently to reflect on his legacy, the *Playboy* founder warmed to the task. "We all now live, to some extent, in a Playboy world," Hefner said. "I can see the effects of the magazine and its campaign for sexual openness everywhere. When [conservative columnist] George Will was here the other day interviewing me, he said, 'You won.' And he's right. It's nice to have gone through the battles with all those Puritans, all those forces of repression and hypocrisy, and to live long enough to see the victory parade."[2]

Here is our silk-pajama-clad grand master overlooking his sweeping victory parade, celebrating his hard-fought campaign for sexual freedom. He believes our sexual circuits were freed by the sexual revolution. But in reality, they've been fried, and our sexual development has been stunted and cut off.

Think back to what I thought about my father's sexuality at Jasen's wedding. I suddenly realized that for all of my father's greatness in sports and business, he had never matured past a junior-high level of control when it came to his sexuality.

Because my father bought in to the Playboy philosophy and never matured in his sexuality, all this "sexual freedom" stuff takes on a dark, personal twist for me. Much of the pain in my life can be traced directly to the doors of *Playboy*'s corporate offices in Chicago. Hefner's sexual revolution convinced my dad that being "tied down" to one wife wasn't cool. So what if he dumped his wife for something more sexually alluring? So what if he had three kids aching to spend time with him, yearning to be loved? At the end of the day, none of that mattered to him.

Instead, my father bought into the Playboy philosophy, openly flaunting his mistresses in my mother's face. I'll never forget playing with my Tonka trucks behind his chair as he typed a love letter to his mistress. I didn't know it at the time, but Mom did. I looked up to see Mom's glazed, sunken eyes riveted on Dad's back, a pair of scissors raised tautly in her right hand. I screamed, and Dad managed to deflect the blow and wrestle the weapon from her hands.

In the months that followed, Dad was vicious, mocking Mom for her childishness and not accepting the new way of the world. But she wouldn't budge. Later, Dad had a lung removed and asked to see his mistress first after the surgery, before Mom. She couldn't take it anymore and divorced him.

A sweeping victory parade? Dad's sexual freedom tipped over our family boat and tossed us into a churning sea of confusion and turbulence. In short, my father slunk away from the family, completely emasculated as our leader. Obsessed with meeting his male "needs" and rejecting the very thing that makes one a genuine man, he embraced irresponsibility, selfishness, and pride. He would never become the servant leader he could have been to us.

Pornography and premarital sex rob you of your destiny. Instead of becoming more of a man, like Jasen did, you become more of a little boy, unable to grow up and grow out of that dominating, selfish fascination with your own sexual desires and impulses. This is what you reap when you toss in your lot with the spirit of Baal, and this is that third swirl of his fingerprint upon our nation: *the reversal of our designed gender roles.*

Look at the marriage of King Ahab and his queen Jezebel, the Bible's poster family of Baal worship. Through Baal, Ahab became the whining, flimsy figurehead of a ruler focused on his selfish desires, while the wicked, seductive Jezebel seized control of the throne and became the ruling head of their family.

This is the key to the confusion currently swirling around our culture. God's design for men and women is for husbands to be heroic as responsible initiators and for wives to be the influential responders. Both are heroic in their sacrifice for the other. But the spirit of Baal turns that pattern on its head. At his altar, the husband is caught up in his lust and disabled as an effective leader, like my father was. Out of her resulting fear and insecurity, the wife is forced to take control of the home, breeding dysfunction and destruction. This is how it was in my family growing up.

We see this same swapping of gender roles in our dating relationships, as well. A young woman once told me that she felt like she cared more about purity than her boyfriend did, although she said he was a great spiritual leader in other areas. "But his leadership doesn't show up in our physical relationship," she said. "We've decided together on boundaries, but he often pushes hard at them. When I resist, he pouts, or asks why I don't desire him physically. I hate making him feel bad and having the blame pushed back on me, so I've gotten very resentful."

Where was her man's heroism? It wasn't her job to defend their boundaries. It was *his* job. God made him the responsible initiator. He may have taken the initiative and set up sexual boundaries, but it's not the act of defining boundaries that makes you a hero. It's the act of defending them. He wasn't responsible, so he wasn't a man, and that forced a role reversal in the relationship. Lust reduces men to mere figureheads, forcing women to take over the leadership to defend their boundaries, leading to resentment, pain, confusion, and ultimately the loss of relationship.

If you set your heart now toward being a hero, to be that responsible initiator, you will take that manhood into your marriage. If not, you'll only be taking your lust and your lies, as another woman described to me in an e-mail. She called herself "desperate" because her husband's porn habit was killing her marriage. "My husband is a believer and knows all the right words to say about this issue, but he can't stop looking at pictures of naked women. He continues to lie to me about it and to deceive himself by saying he 'isn't as bad as the next guy.' We have been to counseling, but that only worked for a day.

"Though I am just married, I have been so completely deceived and lied to that I've become someone else, someone I don't want to be. This is a nightmare compared to my Christian dreams of marriage. I had no idea what I was getting myself into when I said, 'I do.'"

If you're not her hero, you'll be her nightmare. You'll throw smoke, dodge responsibility, and swap gender roles with your girl, making her into something she wasn't meant to be and doesn't want to be.

I keep this e-mail on my desk as a reminder of why I write. It's the direct opposite of the call I once received from Minnesota one month after my son's wedding. My new daughter-in-law, Rose, was on the line, so happy she could barely contain herself. She said to me, "I just wanted to call you to tell you that Jasen is everything you promised he'd be." She gushed, "I'm so happy I could scream."

Will you be her hero or her nightmare?

Focus carefully on that question. I'm not asking it for effect, and I didn't give you an American history lesson to set the stage for some point I'm planning to make later on in the book. Our cultural collapse is the main point, and because of it, you have some important decisions to make.

When it comes to women, will you be a man?

Will you be a hero in this hour of history, when so few have the heart to care?

Let me be frank. The defining moment of your life as a man is upon you, my friend, just as it was for me when I looked into my toddler son's eyes and realized the enormity of the stakes resting upon my next decision. You may be young, but you're a man, and you can choose to be different from those who went before you, just as I chose to be different within my family tree. The stakes are immeasurably high, and many are counting on you.

So far, too few of the men in your generation have stepped up as heroes in their relationships with girls, but that can change quickly if you don't lose sight of the importance of this day. This could be your finest hour, but you must resolutely choose the harder, more heroic path, turning away from sexual indulgence and refusing to shrink from the courageous work at hand.

That's the kind of hero we're all waiting for. Remember, great men are defined by great wars. It's your moment.

Look around. The stage has been set for you. The spirit of Baal has an iron grip on this nation. His fingerprints are everywhere, even in the church. Our men are hobbled, and our women are being abused at his corrupting hands and warped by his polluted touch. Are you going to just sit around and take that? Will you heroically deny yourself and defend the purity of the women around you in God's name or just keep using them for sexual target practice?

You are a man, and that means something. Think back on every plastic weapon you bravely brandished as a boy and every football game against your cross-town rivals and every epic movie that ever captured that male swagger in your soul.

Every male heart yearns for a battle to fight, an adventure to live for, and a beauty to save, and this battle for sexual purity lays all three before you at once. You're built for moments like these, and this is your moment.

If you've missed seeing that before now, it's likely because you've missed who's to blame for the sexual mess around here. God wants you to know who He's holding responsible for all this today, right now. You are responsible, my friend. You, and your generation.

Wait a minute! I wasn't even born yet when Hefner came on the scene.

God isn't saying you're responsible for how the mess got here, but as a group, you're certainly responsible for why it's *still* here, especially within the church. You can't blame the culture or the easy Internet access to porn or the sex-drenched movies that Hollywood cranks out like sausage, any more than I could blame my father or my grandfather for my actions with girls or for the generational curses in my family tree. The fact is, God couldn't have been more clear about that when He laid the responsibility squarely at my feet, asking me, *Are you going to drive the stake into the ground right here and change the destiny of your family tree, or will you be leaving the job for some man better than you, somewhere down the line?*

The failures of those who rode *before* me had no bearing upon my situation as a young, broken father looking desperately into my son's eyes, and they certainly had no place in my conversation with God that day. He couldn't have been more clear. I was the one responsible now.

Sure, my forefathers didn't lead well. When they were faced with their defining moments as men, they failed. Every single one of them was called to be a dangerous warrior-hero for the Lord's kingdom, but when it came to their sexuality, every last one had morphed into weak, intimidated husbands and fathers who kept folding under social pressure and slinking away from their families into porn and their bands of mistresses, totally emasculated as family leaders.

Baal's curse came upon us as a family because of their failures, no doubt about it. But as the last one out of the gene pool, that curse had now become my responsibility, and mine alone. It was *my* battle to be fought and *my* chance to be a hero—to rescue my wife and sons and daughters from the consequences of sexual sin—and I wasn't about to miss it.

Too many men do. In fact, they miss God's whole point about heroic purity. This battle is not just some puny, white-knuckled skirmish to mark out the boundaries on what we can't watch or where we can't touch, and it's not just about slapping our hands when we do or keeping them scrubbed clean of the pleasures of sin until matrimony's cavalry can gallop in to save the day.

No, this is about forging you as a man. This is the battle that defines your manhood, my friend—your ultimate destiny. This battle provides the opportunity to prove to yourself and to the world that you're man enough to be everything your Christian label promises you'll be. It's about choosing to be her hero and not her nightmare, and proving you're man enough to make it stick, through Christ.

By God's grace, I saw this epic battle for what it was. Remember what I said in the last chapter? I knew this was the defining moment of my life and my manhood. I could either "man up" and pick a fight with this brutal taskmaster, or I could drift meekly into the same retreating rabble of Stoeker men and spend the rest of my days merely posing as a man, as they had.

My heart had never been so stirred, and there would be no more posing. I was off to destroy my family's oppressor. I was heading into enemy territory with the mantle of manhood wrapped tightly around my shoulders and the Almighty's charter to conquer the demons of lust that held me shackled in shame. No wonder my heart was soaring. I'd finally found that place in God where I didn't have to turn the other cheek, where real men could strap it on—and where head-butts were definitely in order.

What about you? Wake up from your slumber, my friend. Broad, corrupted fields lay before you, and they are yours to conquer. Get up and face the ruthless oppressor who has devastated your country, emasculating her sons and ravishing her daughters. Defy your satanic oppressors!

Don't keep wringing your hands and murmuring nervously, *Well, those movies aren't really that bad, are they? Why pick a fight over all that? I just want to get along. And will it really hurt anyone if I slip a hand up under her shirt? Nobody's going to get pregnant…no harm, no foul.*

No!

God's looking for real men in His army, not mice. In a family tree, God looks for the man who'll grab a sword and step into that broken gap in their wall to fight off the enemy. In the span of a nation's rise and decline, God looks for the generation that will stand, and He's asking you a similar question to the one He posed to me: *Will it be now, in your generation, or will you leave it to a generation better than yours, somewhere down the line?*

God has a battle for you to fight, for your freedom as sons and for the peace and safety of his daughters. He's not about to walk away from America's mess. He's already out on the field of battle, calling for warriors to join Him there. He will fight with you, and He's not the least bit intimidated by the stakes.

God is up to the challenge. The question is, are you? I believe God will one day raise up a new generation in America that will reject the spirit of Baal and set their eyes on Him alone, just as He raised up this new generation in my own family tree.

Will it be yours? Your defining moment is upon you. He's ready to pour out revival if you'll just mount up together and stop accepting the bankrupt deals of the enemy. Drive that stake in the ground. Date differently. Marry differently. Father differently. As men, you have what it takes because you're made to come through in battle.

Now it's time to prove it. Be men! With God's gifts and His unfailing support, your generation can undo this mess in our country, starting first with the battle in your own heart. This revival starts with you. It must come *to* you before it can come *through* you. Confront the spirit of Baal in your life, right now. Tell him you've got a war to wage with him and that you won't back down for anything—social, emotional, mental, physical, or spiritual.

Is it fair for God to ask a man to live this differently in an American culture so foreign to the ways of Christ? Is it even possible? It's not only possible to live differently…it can even change the very culture you're standing in, as well, as you'll see in the next chapter. All God needs is for a few good men to step into the gap and refuse to bow to sensual idolatry.

You are up to this challenge, my friend. You can walk victoriously through your sex-soaked culture and write your own remarkable story of His grace and blessing, just like Jasen did.

But where do you take that first step? If you want to be a hero to God and to the women in your life, you must head out to purity's party early.

3

IDOL

"Y ou're a greater man than I ever dreamed of being, Son."

A strong statement? Perhaps. But it's indisputable.

Look, I know my son. And as a man, I recognize true manhood when I see it. When it comes to purity with women, Jasen has it. Any guy can keep his hands holy while sitting next to his girl in church. But any red-blooded Christian male parked on this side of puberty understands that nothing takes more grit, guts, and determination than keeping your hands holy from the first date right through to the honeymoon. *That* level of manhood demands the highest degree of respect and honor, which is why Jasen has earned mine, and why his buddies cheered like crazy at his wedding.

Jasen has me trumped. Sure, I'm pure now, but I was late arriving to the purity party. I was forced the hard way to choose that path in the wake of too many far-too-physical relationships with women.

So how did he do it?

I can assure you he wasn't raised in a sheltered home or sealed off in a remote cave. Sex was common among the paired-off couples passing him in the hallways of Johnston High, and the surging tides of sensuality at Iowa State University were swirling just as turbulently as those on any other college campus. Like anyone his age, Jasen knew exactly what was out there, especially as president of his dorm floor during his junior year. In that position, he knew all the gossip and scuttlebutt passing through those residence halls. I'll never forget the time he called near the end of the spring semester to share a dubious milestone: "Dad, except for my roommates and me, every single guy on our floor has had multiple sex partners this year!"

He could have chosen to be part of all that, like many young Christian men do. He just didn't.

It wasn't because he was blessed with an iron will. He's not wired that way. He didn't have some pressing need to protect my reputation as the author of *Every Man's Battle*, either—that wasn't his style. And he never would have lied or covered it up. That's simply not in him.

Jasen's victory came from something far more basic, and far more heroic. He took on the truest mark of manhood early on and never looked back. What mark? His complete willingness to embrace social pain for a higher cause. That gave him the strength to stand against all of the opposition.

That was crucial, because America has lifted an enticing golden idol to another god in this nation, and it's called *Premarital Sex*. Carefully crafted by master sculptors in places like Madison Avenue and delicately polished by Hollywood artisans, Premarital Sex towers across the fruited plain and is visible from sea to shining sea.

Sadly, its allure does not stop at our shores. It's now gone "viral" through the influence of the worldwide media, and today we find many countries suffering the same rising rates of teen pregnancy, abortion, divorce, disease, and porn addiction. Extramarital sex is to blame for most of it, so when it comes to these slipping cultural standards around the world, the evidence is in. Since America is the creator of much of the world's media, our idol has now become the *world's* idol. More and more, the voice of popular culture in *every* country is commanding every last one of us to gather before the gleaming image and bow before it—or catch the tremendous blowback that inevitably follows.

That's the context that makes Jasen's victory all the more remarkable. Though the stakes were impossibly high, Jasen calmly and heroically rejected that command, refusing to bend his knee. How was that possible in this day and age in America, amid all the social pressure? The Bible confirms that it is always possible, no matter what the day or how high the stakes.

The Idol of Babylon

Our worship of the idol of Premarital Sex reminds me of the forced worship of another golden idol erected several thousand years ago in Babylon. Nebuchadnezzar, the brash ruler of one of the greatest kingdoms in the history of the world, ordered a massive statue to be created in his honor. Towering ninety feet above the great plains of Dura in the king's home province, all of the government leaders and provincial officials in the entire kingdom were summoned to attend the enormous dedication ceremony that scholars say was a gorgeous spectacle lasting a whole week. That's how three godly leaders named Shadrach, Meshach, and Abednego found themselves standing out there in the bright, hot sunshine, squinting into the shining face of a gigantic pagan image.

As the throngs of people looked on and all the powerful officials were in their place, the king's herald proclaimed this to the greatest and largest culture in the world at that time:

> This is what you are commanded to do, O peoples, nations and men of
> every language: As soon as you hear the sound of the horn, flute, zither,
> lyre, harp, pipes and all kinds of music, you must fall down and worship
> the image of gold that King Nebuchadnezzar has set up. Whoever does not
> fall down and worship will immediately be thrown into a blazing furnace.
> (Daniel 3:4–6)

The three exiled Jews were among the king's most trusted friends and leaders, and they had managed to serve him loyally with distinction and honor for two decades while remaining faithful to God. But none of that mattered now to the megalomaniac on the throne. King Nebuchadnezzar decreed that *everyone* must bow or face certain death. Shadrach, Meshach, and Abednego refused.

When Nebuchadnezzar caught wind of this, he summoned them in a rage. *Can this be true? My herald couldn't have been any clearer! Who do they think they are?* Perhaps because of their longstanding faithfulness in his courts, he looked the three straight in the eye and offered them a second opportunity to bow before the idol. The trio wouldn't budge. They were real men, and they had a cause—to be God's intimate allies at all times. Respectfully responding to the king's command, Shadrach, Meshach, and Abednego uttered the most courageous words spoken in the entire Old Testament:

> O Nebuchadnezzar, we do not need to defend ourselves before you in this matter. If we are thrown into the blazing furnace, the God we serve is able to save us from it, and he will rescue us from your hand, O king. But even if he does not, we want you to know, O king, that we will not serve your gods or worship the image of gold you have set up. (Daniel 3:16–18)

I was awestruck when I first heard these words as a young Christian. These men's willingness to accept pain for the sake of a higher cause set them apart from that crowd, and most any other crowd, for that matter. Where did that willingness come from? It came from way back, many years before they laid their lives on the line before the king's idol that day.

We know from Scripture that these three young men were among the first mass deportation of Jews to Babylonia when their home country of Judah was besieged for her sins against God. When the Jews finally surrendered, Nebuchadnezzar ordered the best and brightest of Judah to serve in their conqueror's palace, receiving special training in the king's court.

This group of young men from Judah's royal families were assimilated into Babylon's ruling hierarchy. They learned the language and literature, the rites and cultural mores. Handpicked by the chief court official, they were "young men without any physical defect, handsome, showing aptitude for every kind of learning, well informed, quick to understand, and qualified to serve in the king's palace" (Daniel 1:4). After three years of schooling in Nebuchadnezzar's courts, these young men—including Daniel, Shadrach, Meshach, and Abednego— graduated into the king's full-time service.

What an incredible opportunity for the fab four! In spite of their country's defeat, they'd snagged respected positions in Babylon's ruling class, much like they had back home. They soon learned, however, that a serious catch came along with the honor. They and their compatriots would be challenged to cut a few corners regarding their covenants with God.

THE FIRST CUT IS THE DEEPEST

In Babylonian culture, the first portions of the roasted meat were offered to idols at pagan altars, which was contrary to the law of Moses. In addition, the animals were neither slaughtered nor prepared according to Mosaic Law, so for Daniel, Shadrach, Meshach, and Abednego, eating this unclean meat was abhorrent, especially in light of Judah's recent crushing defeat. After all, cutting corners with God was the very reason they'd lost their homes in the first place.

Surprisingly, their Jewish colleagues hadn't learned that lesson in spite of all they'd been through, and there was genuine pressure to go along to get along. *Hey, we lost. Get over it! We're in Babylon now. God chose to assimilate us, right? Quit rocking the boat.*

But these four heroes were resolute.

Knowing they faced possible dismissal from the king's court and social suicide with their Jewish brothers, the fab four still refused to defile themselves with the choice food at the king's table. To them, it wasn't about food. They had a mission, written in the very fabric of their hearts. They were going to be God's heroes, no matter where they landed, and they had dedicated their lives to that transcendent cause.

"Test us," they said, offering a counterproposal. "Let us eat our foods for ten days and see how we measure up to everyone else."

And after ten days, Daniel and the others "looked healthier and better nourished" (Daniel 1:15) than their counterparts, and by God's grace, they deflected that early bullet. We're also told that God poured out blessings on them because of their stand, granting them "wisdom and understanding"—in supernatural quantities—that made them so valuable to Nebuchadnezzar's court that "he found them ten times better than all the magicians and enchanters in his whole kingdom" (Daniel 1:20).

Then twenty years passed. Out of nowhere, King Nebuchadnezzar ordered everyone to bow before his golden image. This time, there was no out. Either they bowed or they'd be cast into the fiery furnace.

It didn't matter that Nebuchadnezzar had ramped the stakes up to the moon this time around. Their decision had already been made two decades before. They were God's men, in life or in death, in fame or in flames. When it came to God and His purposes in their lives, they were *all in*, just as they'd always been. Their miraculous stand before the thousands on the plain of Dura was actually born years earlier when they settled their identity as God's heroes during the confusing social turbulence in their youth.

Have you made that same early decision today, in the present social turbulence of *your* youth? You'll never face a blazing furnace for refusing to bow before America's idol, but you'll certainly experience the heat of ridicule, rejection, and possible social excommunication for ignoring that loud command to join the sexual revelry with your girlfriend. Will you stand, or will you bow?

Your answer to this question will be found in your answer to the first one: Is your identity settled in the one true God, or have you been making your own inimitable little bow before the idol by exploring her body in ways the Lord could never smile upon, using exploration techniques you would never risk if her dad was in the next room gripping a thirty-six-ounce Louisville Slugger in his hands?

If you've been fooling around physically with your girlfriend, let's face it, my friend. You've lost your way. You were created to run with God and to be His intimate ally in a great cosmic war, not to be some girl's intimate pet. You've sold out as a man.

The fab four were real men, and if you want to be like them, you must dedicate your life to be God's hero, no matter what your situation. They were completely willing to embrace and endure any social pain in their pursuit of God and godly character, and you'll require that same willingness if you're to maintain your sexual purity while dating.

After all, you'll catch it good when you stand up for God's ways. You'll hear friends whispering, "Why isn't he doing it? Sex is so natural!" Others will shake their heads in pity, murmuring, "Boy, look at all the fun he's missing." Some will snicker behind your back, "Sheltered dweeb! Mama's boy! Homo!" Some will even mock you to your face.

Our culture is what it is, and it certainly isn't Christian these days. That's why the willingness to embrace social pain is not just the place where manhood begins, but also the place where your purity begins. There will be heat, and that's a given. Will you make an early decision to be God's hero, no matter what, even in the face of that heat? If not, your heart and courage will melt before the social flames. Let me show you how that looks in real life with this story.

Tom, a high school freshman, couldn't wait for the football season to start. Sure, he knew that ramming tackling sleds and racing up hills in full pads under a broiling sun in the middle of August would be the toughest thing he'd ever endured, but he craved the camaraderie of being with the guys and being part of a team. There was something about squaring off and pounding each other into the freshly cut grass that formed deep bonds with his teammates.

As the sweaty squad turned on the showers after their first practice, the talk naturally turned to girls. Tom told the guys about Jenna, whom he'd been dating since early June.

"Is that all you've been doing—going out with her?" smirked one of the linemen, a junior, and the rest of the team laughed at Tom's expense.

"Well…yes, I guess so," replied Tom, who felt embarrassed. They had kissed a little after hitting the theater a few times, but that was it. As members of the same youth group, they'd already talked things through, and they agreed that was as far as they wanted to go for now.

"His equipment must be broken, huh, guys?" said the lineman.

"Or maybe it isn't there at all!" shouted the starting quarterback, the charismatic team leader. "What do ya say, Tom-Girl?" Everyone erupted in laughter, and Tom wished he could shrivel up and blow away.

Over the next few weeks, "The Voice" got louder and louder, teasing Tom incessantly about "how far he was getting" with Jenna. He wanted to make something up to get them off his back, but he was afraid it would get back to

Jenna and, besides, that would invite the inevitable follow-up questions: Was she hot? Did she fight it?

Maybe there's something wrong with me, Tom reasoned. *If everyone else on the football team is having sex except for me, what does that say about me?* As a freshman, Tom wanted desperately to belong as a member of the Rams football team, the third-ranked team in the state in the preseason polls.

I'll never belong if I keep acting so girly, Tom mused to himself. *I know what God says about premarital sex, but if these guys don't respect me, I'll never get to hang out with them, and if I'm not with them, I can't witness to them or bring them to church.*

Tom was confused, but one thing was crystal clear: all he had to do was bow to that towering golden idol, and he would become one of the boys, one of the initiated.

So Tom increased the pressure on Jenna slowly but surely, breaking down her resistance bit by bit, date by date. On a couple of occasions, he tested her by touching her in places their youth pastor told him never to touch. When she asked him to stop, he did, but after a respite, he went back to work. Soon, her resistance was fading fast.

One Sunday afternoon, Tom found himself all alone with Jenna at her house after her parents had left for the mall with her kid brother. Four weeks of pounding had left Jenna's defenses exhausted, and now Tom saw nothing but daylight between him and the end zone.

The next afternoon after practice, Tom told his teammates about the "hot time" he'd had in Jenna's bedroom over the weekend. War whoops echoed through the showers, and the looks of admiration from his teammates delivered the only message he wanted to hear, loud and clear: *You're in, Tom. You're finally one of the boys.*

Tom's knees had buckled before the idol of Premarital Sex, and while that made him quite the stud to his teammates, he was certainly no hero. He hadn't demonstrated the slightest trace of true manhood before God or shown one bit of willingness to embrace social pain for Jenna's sake.

How can you become the hero God calls you to be with women? You begin by living that uncompromised life for the Lord early, right now, even *before* you begin your next relationship. Tom didn't do that, but Jasen did. He'd planted the seeds for purity with girls long before he even cared about dating them, in much the same way Shadrach, Meshach, and Abednego had planted the seeds for their victory long before the king built his idol. You'll never be willing to embrace social pain for your girlfriend later on if you're not used to embracing social pain for Him now.

Jasen learned early to embrace that pain for the Lord. Let me share a portion of his story to show you how that looks in practice.

CLOSE ENCOUNTER

I came up with the plan to read through *Preparing for Adolescence* with Jasen when he turned eleven because I knew that puberty would soon dump mental and emotional anguish all over him. I hadn't forgotten how puberty messed up my life, and so I was excited for this chance to pass on what I knew about what awaited him.

But butterflies danced in my stomach as I headed for his bedroom that first night. I wasn't exactly sure how to talk to an eleven-year-old about sex. I was pretty certain I'd be hit with that dreaded sigh and the roll of the eyes in response to my offer.

I sat on his bed and showed him the book. After he paused his Game Boy, I said, "Jasen, I think it's time we go through this book together. I know this might feel a little uncomfortable, but you will soon be entering a very interesting period of development."

"Oh yeah," he said. "I've heard of that. It's called *perverty*, right?"

I suppressed a laugh. "It's actually *puberty*, Big Guy." I paused and let the chuckle escape. "But your word might be a better fit, come to think of it."

Pushing ahead, I proceeded. "Puberty's going to bring on some mental and emotional changes, Jace. It is hard for me to put those into words exactly, but let me try. You'll likely soon experience more peer pressure from your friends, and you might even care more about your friends' opinions than mine for a while. The other kids will be trying to find their way through this at the same time, so you'll likely face some hurts and embarrassments. Everyone will be pushing and pulling and climbing over you on their way up the pecking order, trying to find spots in the most popular groups. I just want to prepare you for it, Son, so you aren't caught off guard."

His response bowled me over. "Dad, I really think it's good that we're going to read this book together, especially right now," he said.

Dumbfounded, I could only stare at him. *Where was that roll of the eyes? that dreaded sigh?* I was speechless for a moment, but I gathered enough of my senses to blurt, "What do you mean?"

"Well, I've been kind of scared lately."

Scared? My son, scared? We lived in a nice, quiet state called Iowa where nothing scary ever happens. "Scared about what?"

"It's just that it's been harder and harder for me to say 'no' to my friends lately. I've been kind of scared—it's been harder for me to stand up to them."

Did you catch what he said? There it was, that voice of the culture, right there on the lips of his peers, calling on him to dump his convictions and be like them. You've heard it too, haven't you? That same voice first calls out to everyone at about the same time, usually around sixth grade.

That's when my daughter Rebecca received her first call. Just a year before, in fifth grade, it didn't matter if people's clothes were old-fashioned or they got bad grades. Everyone belonged. Everyone was friends, and no one made fun of each other or cared about their differences.

That all changed overnight. When she hit sixth grade, her friends began to break into cliques, and some of her friends who used to talk to her and invite her over for sleepovers were now dissing her. "I see so many kids without friends, and so many people getting cut off from everyone else," she told me.

Yup, things change quickly in the middle school years, but that's the point of the early decision. The heat ramps up quickly, so you need to be ready. Only a few weeks after Jasen and I had discussed his fears, his friends called him over to take a peek at that *Hustler* magazine. Ignoring their chatter, he refused to bow.

That encounter was just the first in a long list of times that Jasen's friends and peers tried to soften his resistance with social pressure. Each time he stood for righteousness, he took a verbal hit that threw him for a social loss. But he'd get up, dust himself off, and keep on playing. He didn't bow, but he did plant the seeds for purity with his girlfriends by getting used to embracing social pain for the Lord. Remember, you can only endure that social pain for the sake of your girlfriend's purity if you're used to enduring such pain as the Lord's hero, both around the school and in your locker rooms.

You Play How You Practice

The foundation for that kind of strength is obviously laid in the off-season, so to speak, when nobody is looking and nobody is cheering. This recently became abundantly clear to me one Friday afternoon in late October. My sophomore son, Michael, and his Dragon teammates were spitting fire as they stormed into Valley Stadium to take on their fiercest rivals, the Dowling Catholic Maroons. Sadly, that would be the best they would look all afternoon. After two possessions, Dowling led 14–0.

As our defense trotted to the sideline following the PAT, our team leader, Paul Farber, exploded. Ripping off his helmet, he flailed his arms and stomped up and down the sideline in a rage. "C'mon, guys! This is embarrassing! Let's go, Dragons!"

I love Paul. I'd have given my left arm to have ten guys just like him on my high school team, but I couldn't help chuckling. "Paul, Paul, Paul…you think it's embarrassing now? Wait until the fourth quarter."

Final score: 41–7.

Did I get a word from the Lord? Nope. But I could see something clearly from the bleachers that Paul hadn't yet recognized on the field. Dowling was quicker, faster, and, most of all, stronger. While I appreciate good fighting spirit as much as the next guy, I knew the game was over midway through the first quarter.

Paul's tantrum didn't bother me because I have a linebacker's heart. I love that spirited, blistering passion. It was the pointlessness that got me. The time for shouting was *the previous December*, to get the players into the weight room and working on speed drills. Paul's inspirational storm could have really accomplished something then, nine months *before* his Dragons stood chagrined on the sidelines, slower and weaker than their opponents, their fire dwindling in their bellies.

It's the same way with purity. Champions are born in the off-season, and you *will* play how you practice. You'd better get used to looking different from the crowd *long before* you're with her, or your character will prove downright embarrassing on the field.

Purity starts with taking on that mark of manhood—that willingness to embrace suffering—in the off-season. Are you all in for God? Nothing predicts victory in the battle for purity better than the heroic heart of an uncompromised life, a heart completely willing to embrace social pain for the higher call. That's the level of manhood young men rarely find, but those who do find it train for it early. That's why no one can make them bow at crunch time.

Long before my son Jasen met his bride, he quietly but heroically aligned his will with his Father's, in spite of the risky cultural crosscurrents. He refused to see his single years as his "practice time" with the girls, because God didn't see those years as practice time. He wasn't confused by his Father's call to purity or bothered by its difficulty, because he trusted the Lord and calmly accepted that call as God's preparation for his future victory. That's why, even as the social heat was rising several notches around him and producing some painful blisters, nothing intimidated him.

And you know what? That same kind of heroic heart lies within you too, given by the Lord, at birth. John Eldredge, in his book *Wild at Heart*, famously put it this way:

> There are three desires I find written so deeply into my heart I know now I
> can no longer disregard them without losing my soul. They are core to who
> and what I am and yearn to be.... I am convinced these desires are

universal, a clue into masculinity itself. They may be misplaced, forgotten, or misdirected, but in the heart of every man is a desperate desire for a battle to fight, an adventure to live, and a beauty to rescue.[1]

Jasen had found his battle to fight and his adventure to live in God, and once his heroic male heart caught destiny's fire, he wasn't looking back. Like Daniel and his friends, Jasen resolved early to be God's warrior, giving his life over to that transcendent cause. That's what it takes to stand up before America's idol.

The good news is that heroism is your birthright as a man. You've been given the same challenge, the same battle to fight, the same soaring adventure to live. And because of that birthright, you've got what it takes to come through.

The bad news is that I've heard from hundreds of young men who admitted they *didn't* stand up before America's idol. Instead, they bowed, choosing to play it safe socially and to risk nothing for their purity. The stakes seemed too high when it came to God's purposes in their lives, but now they're living with the pain of regret and a seared conscience. This e-mail is a fairly typical one:

I once wrote to you about my struggles with purity back in high school, but today I'm writing because I just reread the first chapter of *Every Young Man's Battle* and, sadly, it sounds a lot like me. At one time I was a pure Christian man, but now I feel so sick, so dirty, like a pig. I'm twenty-two and in my last year of college in Ohio, and I desperately want to be a man of God, but it is really hard to do when I'm sleeping around and constantly giving myself away to women I barely know.

It just tears me apart. My relationship with Christ is gradually slipping into hell, and my identity in Him is something I don't even know anymore. I can't begin to express how deeply I'm hurting right now. Lately it's been pretty common for me to just randomly break down and cry.

That's the life you're ordered to accept by those calling you to bow down before their idol, my friend. Some life!

I've lived that life. It's far better to stand up bravely and to be thrown into a fiery social furnace than to live like that. If saving your social skin is your focus and sexual pleasure your primary aim, you've abandoned your place on His battle lines and chosen not to fight. You've surrendered your heart to the enemy and become his prisoner, and when it comes to your dating relationships, nothing transcendent is inspiring your life or defining you as a man.

You don't have to live that way. You can live heroically and draw a line in the sand, refusing to bow—yes, even here, even in our culture. Sure, choosing to be God's hero risks everything for you socially, just as it did for Daniel, Shadrach, Meshach, and Abednego, but at least your identity will be settled completely in God. You may become a target of ridicule, but you'll be learning to stand heroically for the Lord in the heat of the off-season, and that training will help you refuse to bow when the game is on, even after falling hopelessly in love with the gorgeous woman God intends just for you.

Jasen is living proof. You can make a firm stand in an antagonistic culture if you're willing to accept loss for the sake of His gain. You saw how that looked in practice with the fab four in ancient Babylon. What would such a stand look like today, in your "Babylon"? You can learn a lot about that from Jasen's own "exile" into a foreign culture we call public school. You can also learn how to train in the off-season to prepare for the dating game. Listen to Jasen as he shares how his purity with Rose began long before they met—all the way back in middle school.

ENTERING BABYLON

From Jasen:

I'll never forget the gasp from the crowd when Pastor Dave announced that Rose and I would be sharing our first kiss at the altar that day. The thunderous applause for that long, firm kiss remains the highlight of my life. What a day! The big, teary hug from my dad meant everything to me, because no one but Dad can understand the depth of discipline it took for me to get to the finish line with Rose. Still, the whoops and high-fives from my buddies at the reception were priceless too. After all, I remember a time when I didn't even have a friend to eat lunch with at school, let alone one to stand up with me at my wedding.

It didn't start out lonely for me, of course. As my dad alluded to earlier, nearly everyone is popular in elementary school, and most everyone gets along. My teachers liked me, my classmates liked me, their parents liked me—things couldn't have been going any better for me.

But what a difference a summer makes. When I stepped into junior high for the first day of seventh grade—bam! I suddenly had no friends, and my old buddies from sixth grade weren't in any of my classes. And even worse, my seventh-grade classmates, including many I had gotten along with just fine previously, soon began to derive great pleasure from making fun of me.

At first, I didn't understand what was happening, but their remarks soon made their intentions clear enough. I didn't know it at the time, but I found out later that I'd been blindsided by the Piaget Effect. Jean Piaget, a brilliant Swiss thinker and psychologist, found that the human brain undergoes dramatic changes as children enter adolescence. Children suddenly begin thinking abstractly about God, life, rules, and relationships for the first time, and heavy questions pop up out of nowhere. For many young guys, some of these top the list:

- Who am I?
- Where do I fit around here?
- How do men think?
- Am I like the other guys, or not?

For seventh graders, this newfound obsession to reflect on big thoughts is in full bloom, and it's serious business, bringing with it a manic search for identity and a strong desire to land a prominent spot on the social ladder. To me, the entire student body seemed to have discovered cliques at the same time, and the subsequent jostling for position in the popular groups crushed many beneath the grinding wheels of change.

It was no secret in my public middle school that I wasn't cool, but I progressed from uncool to seriously uncool the first time my English teacher popped a PG-13 film in to use as a teaching tool. Since my parents hadn't yet reviewed this particular film, and since I knew most PG-13 movies had some seriously sensual language along with a sprinkling of sexual situations and partial nudity, the odds were good that some audio and visual pollution was heading my way. I decided on the spot that I couldn't afford to stay in my seat. Heading quickly to the teacher's desk, I quietly said, "I'm not comfortable watching this movie because I don't think the content will be appropriate for me as a Christian. I just don't want this stuff in my head, so if it's okay with you, I'll sit out in the hallway."

My English teacher registered a look of surprise, but she nodded her okay. The whole class stared in stunned silence as I walked out of the classroom.

I knew what they were thinking: Why in the world would you do something stupid like that?

But to me, the decision to step outside was no more stupid than Daniel asking for a pass from eating the unclean foods at King Nebuchadnezzar's table. Since when is obedience stupid? If what I did seemed strange to the "Babylonians" attending my school, that's no surprise to me. Most people—and that includes our brothers and sisters in Christ—have been living in Babylon so long their thinking has been warped and they're no longer able to recognize what's sensible in God's kingdom. Since God says that I'm not to have even a hint of sexual immorality in my life (Ephesians 5:3), and since a guy can't stay in the classroom and avoid overhearing the sensual conversations in those films, I had no alternative. By God's instruction, it was time for *every* Christian in that classroom to excuse himself and sit in the hallway.

Now, you're probably thinking my dad put me up to this, right? If so, you'd be wrong. I wasn't thinking about what he would think—that didn't factor in at all. I didn't have time to consult him, and that wouldn't have changed what I did anyway. I knew what God expected of me, so I did it. From that first time in seventh grade to my senior year at Johnston High, I must have asked to skip watching several dozen films, and each time it was my decision, and mine alone.

My teachers typically had no problem with me sitting out in the hall or going to the library during a movie, and I didn't mind having the extra study time. I'd read a book or get a jump on my homework.

I didn't get off quite that easy with my classmates, though. I could count on every last one staring at me as I left the classroom, and usually a few snickers too. One time when I stood up to approach the teacher, one jock gave me a verbal forearm to the jaw in front of the whole class. "You aren't thirteen yet? Why can't you watch PG-13 movies?"

But the heaviest verbal shots were delivered *after* class, out of the teacher's earshot. Gratefully, every so often someone would be genuinely curious: "Dude, why did you leave like that?" While most didn't get what I was doing, a few—very few—responded in an entirely different manner. "That's pretty cool. I really respect your decision."

EVERY RULE CHANGED

Looking back on those days, I see striking similarities between the Jewish exile into Babylon and the typical entry into seventh grade. As young teens, Daniel,

Shadrach, Meshach, and Abednego had been popular members of Judah's future ruling elite. Suddenly, they were marched into exile and forced to assimilate into a foreign culture where every rule of behavior had changed and nobody saw things like they did anymore.

Sound familiar? Through sixth grade, everyone's popular until those few, bright weeks of summer give way to a one-lane highway into exile, and we're tossed into a turbulent culture that's clearly antagonistic to all we are...or should be.

Political or social, exile always demands an early decision from a child of God, no matter how unfair it seems at the time. *Should I grab a rung on the social ladder and allow the others to define who I am? Or should I remain who I am in God and ride out whatever storms come my way?*

One choice carries disturbing spiritual risks, while the other brings frightening social ones. My younger sister Rebecca summarized the risks pretty well while adjusting to her own exile into seventh grade. "I had the chance to get into one of the popular cliques," she said. "But right away I felt uneasy. In the popular cliques, you aren't free. If someone in the group dislikes a person outside the group, you have to dislike that person too. You've got to think and behave like the rest of the group all the time, even if it seems like the wrong thing to do. Being popular is kind of like being in prison."

Rebecca saw through the veneer: there's no way to be popular in public school without compromise. Which leads each of us to the pulse-quickening question: do I give in to keep the voices of the other kids quiet, or do I stand on my own with God?

I couldn't do both—no man can. I couldn't remain pure and godly if I clung to the popular standards regarding movies. And yet if I didn't go along and watch those movies, I wasn't going to be popular. That was pretty much all there was to it.

It was the same with dating, a topic I knew nothing about in middle school. Since no one could drive, a middle school "date" meant that a guy took a girl to the vending machine and bought her a Coke, or each parent dropped their child off at a theater, where they shared popcorn and held hands until their parents came to pick them up afterward.

Why kids spent so much time worrying about such lame dates was beyond me. But lame or not, I was doomed on that one too, because you had to date to be popular. Trouble is, my parents had already made it clear I wasn't to "date" until I was sixteen. If I wanted to do right, I'd obey my parents. If I wanted to be popular, I'd have to date behind my parents back. No matter how I looked at it, I'd have to compromise the things I believed in to be popular. If I wanted to stop the insults, I'd have to bow.

You're always free to make your own choices in Babylon. You just aren't free to have it both ways.

So, faced with this stark reality, I opted out of the cliques and social ladders in middle school with a heroic decision. I chose God over cool.

I must confess that I didn't *feel* particularly heroic at the time, however. Those weren't fun years, and I don't long to relive them. In fact, they were unsettling times marked by risky decisions that I barely felt old enough to make. I'm sure Daniel and his friends must have felt the same way when they were dumped into Babylon during their teen years. Like them, I'd chosen a heroic path from God's point of view, but practically no one else saw it that way. People were still making fun of me, and the teasing and snide comments were painful.

Still, I had one thing going for me. I had made a man's decision, and better yet, I knew exactly who I was. I was a young man with standards, and while that didn't keep the loneliness away, it eliminated any of the deeper confusion in my life.

Once I made that decision to step outside the classroom while a PG-13 movie was shown, heroic choices became easier, almost as a matter of course. To my great surprise, because of my stand, God was about to bless me with something quite unexpected.

An awesome group of friends.

The Crowd and the Cafeteria

Because our school system was growing like a weed, our middle school building became too small to fit the entire seventh grade into the cafeteria at lunchtime.

The administration's solution was simple enough. During the thirty-minute lunch period, half the grade would sit in the gymnasium for fifteen minutes while the other half ate, and then the two groups would switch to allow the rest to grab their lunch.

Administratively, this may have been a brilliant solution, but it was downright devastating to me emotionally. The two groups were divided alphabetically, and my one or two friends left over from sixth grade were in the other half of the alphabet. Now I had to face the dreaded lunchtime completely on my own.

Every day I sat by myself in the loneliest corner of the gym, while the other kids were gathered in bunches, talking and laughing. It was excruciating from the start, but after a few weeks of withering isolation, those thirty minutes became absolutely intolerable.

Something had to change. I couldn't face eating lunch by myself another day, let alone the next six years. With nothing to lose, I decided to take a risk. I figured I couldn't be the only one sitting alone in there. I looked around the gymnasium and spotted a couple of kids sitting in the opposite corner. No one else seemed to be paying them much attention, either. Swallowing hard, I stood up and walked over to introduce myself. "Hey, guys, how you doing? I'm Jasen. What's your names?"

They looked up in surprise, wondering how I could see them when they were clearly invisible to everyone else. "Jack," one responded. "I'm Rob," said the other. It was an inauspicious start, but soon after, we were talking all things Nintendo, and before long, our daily fifteen minutes in the gym became a standing date for Nintendo 64 tip swapping. One day, they happened to mention their two friends, Rich and Don, from the other half of the alphabet. When I heard their names called in PE the next day, I quickly went over to meet them. Before we knew it, we were facing down the world in dodge ball, shoulder to shoulder, back to back.

Things were definitely looking up for me, and I kept my foot on the gas in my search for other outcasts, guys or girls who hadn't quite made popularity's grade. I found a couple more sitting in advanced classes, too smart for their social good. A few more had been cut off because of their average looks or their style tastes. Soon I'd pulled together around a dozen, forming an awesome, diverse group of incredible guys and girls. Some were Christians, some weren't, but together we formed the finest bunch of friends any guy could imagine.

My dad said it was the bravest thing he'd ever seen a guy do, adding, "Jasen, I remember vividly what the pain of junior high was like, so I can practically feel what you were feeling as you sat there alone in your little corner of the gym. I can't even imagine what it took for you to look around for the other lonely guys, and then to scrape up the courage to step right up to them to introduce yourself. There was so much risk of rejection, and you were already feeling rejected before you even crossed that floor. I don't think I could have done that. That took real guts, Jasen."

His words meant the world to me, but at the time, it didn't seem so heroic. After all, I could only see two alternatives. What's so heroic about choosing the least painful one? Granted, I could have been rejected by those guys, but to me that was far better than sitting alone in that corner until school ended in June. I suppose there was a third option. I could have ingratiated myself with the cool kids—hanging out on weekends, going to their movies, maybe even seeing a girl or two behind my parents' backs. But I'd already dismissed that option. If reaching out to other outcasts was heroic, it was because I chose risking rejection over accepting the cool crowd's more comfortable and mediocre standards.

Following the path of least resistance in the school hallways definitely would have been the easy way, but Daniel, Shadrach, Meshach, and Abednego feared that path, and so should we. It's one thing to move into Babylon and try to fit in as best you can. It's quite another to compromise your principles in God, because when you compromise, you rob God's ability to bless you.

Consider what He's doing in heaven right now. His eyes are running to and fro over the whole earth, looking for someone on whose behalf He can show His power, as it says in 2 Chronicles 16:9. Who is He looking for? He's looking for the one whose heart is fully committed to Him, the one who's being faithful in both the little and the big things, like sexual purity. He's looking for guys who will stand in the gap for Him on behalf of our sensual culture, ones who will help rebuild our crumbling walls through their uncompromised obedience to His Word (Ezekiel 22:30), and who are willing to accept the true mark of manhood: to embrace personal pain for His purposes.

I've seen many guys my age step *away* from manhood and run from the social pain, covering their tracks with the excuse that they're trying to help the non-Christian students feel more comfortable with Christianity so they'll find God more attractive.

That musty old song has been playing for centuries. Most of the Jews chosen for Nebuchadnezzar's court program were probably crooning right along, rationalizing their "reasonable" compromises that allowed them to stay out of trouble and fit right in with *their* popular crowd, the ruling elite of Babylon. In fact, I can hear one of them now:

Guys, we have a great opportunity right now to influence Nebuchadnezzar's court for God—if we don't offend them with our beliefs. We need to make God attractive to them, so here's the deal. If we just let the food regulations slide a little bit, we could avoid giving God, and ourselves, a bad name. This is how we can reach them with the truth!

I sure hope those fanatics—Daniel, Shadrach, Meshach, and Abednego—don't do us in and take us down with them. We're just being salt and light to these Babylonians, right?

The Babylonians didn't need just a pinprick of light and a pinch of salt sprinkled into their culture by a few new "Jewish flavored" Babylonians. They needed men who would *be* Jews, and who would live out the entire uncompromised truth, so that their king's advisors would be blessed by God. Since God doesn't bless mixture and compromise, what they *really* needed was for all of the Jews in the assimilation program to be heroic for God and to live uncompromised lives.

Since only four were up to the challenge, Babylon only got four advisors blessed of God.

The truth is what Babylon needed, and that's what the culture at your school needs. God doesn't need your help to make Him more attractive, nor does He need your spiritual compromises in order to bless those around you. He needs you to stand up heroically and to live an uncompromised life, presenting His uncompromised truth in an uncompromised way. If you do, it will impact your culture's destiny, and it will impact your destiny too.

DESTINY'S CHILD

Daniel's early commitment to the uncompromised life as a teenager certainly affected *his* entire destiny, which may surprise you. We often view the teen years as a time of dodging responsibility to have a little fun before the drudgery of real life begins. While there's nothing wrong with carefree times in life, it's a lie to believe that your teenage decisions carry little impact upon your future.

What if Daniel had taken the easy route, compromising with the larger, more popular group of Jews instead of sticking with Shadrach, Meshach, and Abednego? If he had, he wouldn't have been blessed with the supernatural power to interpret Nebuchadnezzar's dream later on, and without that gift, all of the Jewish leaders in Babylon would have been killed, including Daniel. When King Darius took over Babylon, Daniel would not have been around to be tossed into the lions' den and be miraculously saved, a jaw-dropping event that transformed King Darius's heart and soul. Later, when the time of the Jewish exile neared its end, Daniel wouldn't have been there to intercede for their release from captivity. It can be said that the destinies of three nations—Babylon, Medo-Persia, and Judah—were impacted by Daniel's willingness, as a teenager, to embrace pain for the sake of God's purposes in his life.

Just as the Jewish exiles needed Daniel to stand up early for God, the Lord needs you to stand up now before *your* Babylonians, whether at your school or at work. The teen and young adult years mattered in Daniel's life, and they matter in your life today.

Now, that doesn't mean it's too late to take that heroic stand if you are past your teen years. The uncompromised life always turns the tumblers toward God, unlocking your destiny in Him. No matter what your age, you still have this day before you; there's a destiny to be written. God's eyes are going to and fro looking for someone to bless, so stand up straight so He can spot you.

My dad is a perfect example. As Dad mentioned, he arrived late to purity's party, and when it came to girls, he made all the wrong decisions in high school and college. He didn't take an uncompromised stand on sexual purity until after he was married. Still, once he did, he refused to bow anymore. God spotted that and gave him an unexpected destiny.

At the time, Dad was a young husband and father, struggling over his distance from God and wondering if his sexual sin was the culprit. The "Babylonian" Christians surrounding him, steeped in compromise, argued that ogling bikinied babes and fantasizing about other women was no big deal. "Oh, come on!" they said. "Nobody can control his eyes and mind, for heaven's sakes. Relax, Fred. That's just how guys are."

But he knew it *was* possible to flee sexual immorality entirely, or God wouldn't have called His sons to do so (1 Corinthians 6:18–20). He knew it *was* possible to live without a hint of sexual immorality in his life, no matter how sensual his surroundings (see Ephesians 5:3). What would have happened had he not made that decision to stand?

For starters, there would have been no testimony in Dad's life. With no testimony, he couldn't have taught his sexual purity classes in Sunday school with any authority or insight. Without teaching those Sunday school classes, there wouldn't have been scores of men telling him he should write a book. Without writing a book, there never would have been *Every Man's Battle*. His books have now sold millions and have been translated into more than thirty languages around the world. Because Dad obeyed God and took an unpopular stand, he changed the destiny of his life, his marriage, and his children, as well as the untold number of destinies of people who have heard Dad speak or have read one of his books.

Look, I just graduated from college. I know how hard it is to think in terms of destiny there. Destinies are measured decade by decade, while pain and loneliness are measured day by day, week by week. No wonder your place in the social ladder at school can command your attention so easily.

But you know something? As young as I am, I can already see the dramatic effects my early decision has had on my destiny. What if I'd decided to compromise my standards in exchange for friends? I would have robbed God of the opportunity to provide me that wonderful group of friends who did *not* pressure my standards at every turn.

He couldn't have used me as well to bless those friends, either. I remember riding in the car one night with my buddy Will, and I happened to have a copy of Dad's book *Preparing Your Son for Every Man's Battle* with me. I mentioned that the book had just won a Gold Medallion award, and Will responded, "Any guy who can raise a son like you deserves a gold medal." Will confirmed that my decisions made an impact in his life.

I'm also dead certain that I would have struggled with my purity with girls throughout high school and college, like practically every other Christian guy my age, if I hadn't made that early decision to opt out. I'd have had no victorious testimony to share, so Dad wouldn't have thought to ask me to speak with him at Glen Eyrie in Colorado. Without that opportunity, Dad would not have asked me to coauthor this book, and I wouldn't have this opportunity to share my story.

Do you know the wildest thing I've learned about these early decisions? When we avoid these decisions for God, compromising our standards and our destiny to gain popularity and to avoid pain, it never works out for us in the long run anyway. Opting out was painful for me at first, but one of the most amazing things I found out at college was that even those who *were* popular at Johnston High had their share of pain back then too. A lot of my high school classmates ended up at Iowa State University like I did, and whenever we talked about those high school days, they'd admit they were being made fun of too.

Even the top athletes and highest achievers at Johnston took a beating. I always thought their social rank made them immune to the mocking and pain, but I guess I'd been wrong, and hearing that made me realize that the whole popularity process had been worthless from the get-go. Everyone catches grief in school, and there is no way out of it, no matter what you sell out. Had I compromised my Christian standards to find a higher place on the social ladder to save myself all the pain, it wouldn't have worked anyway. Compromise would have simply torpedoed my destiny, and I'd have gotten nothing in exchange for the loss.

Pressure Is a Privilege

I was never much into sports—unless you consider paintball a sport (which it is). Though my only sport in high school was swimming, I still think we can learn a lot from athletics. Once, when I was complaining about how hard our workouts were in the pool, Dad repeated a quote from an Iowa Hall of Fame wrestling coach named Bob Darrah, who said, "You will always have pain in life, men, but at least you get to choose between two kinds—the pain of self-discipline or the pain of regret. Choose well, but remember this. The pain of self-discipline lasts for a moment. The pain of regret lasts for the rest of your life."

I imagine his words played great in the wrestling room, but they play extremely well in the dating game too. For instance, when it comes to women, I'll never grapple with the pain of regret. Like champion wrestlers, I embraced the pain of self-discipline in middle school instead, and I left it all on the mat when it came to my relationships. I'll never have to wonder, *What might have happened had I just walked with God completely in my sexuality and in my relationships with women?* I already know what might have been because I *did* walk with Him completely, and it was worth every disciplined moment.

Sure, I also suffered loss, but that's a given. Self-discipline and social loss always go hand in hand in a sensual nation like ours. The real variable in the dating equation will be this one: Are you man enough to step up to Christ's shoulder to gain all that He's promised His obedient warriors? Will you lay everything on the line for Him in order to protect His girls?

Look, if you end up touching your girlfriend in places you shouldn't and kissing her so heavily that you're driven to distraction by the memories when you get back to your room later that night, it won't be because God has somehow failed you. He has given you everything you need to walk purely with her (2 Peter 1:3–4). You have what it takes.

If you fail, it's because you haven't yet decided to stand and protect the women in your life, and you haven't yet taken all He's given you and laid it back on the line for Him, with everything you've got. In short, when it comes to girls, you haven't chosen manhood. It's time to risk obedience.

My dad tells me that before tennis star Maria Sharapova captured the Australian Open singles championship in 2008, the great champion Billie Jean King sent her an encouraging text message, reminding her, "Champions take chances, and pressure is a privilege."[1]

I encourage you with these same words as you fight for your destiny. You are meant to be a champion of God, and champions take chances, like taking on the self-disciplined, uncompromised life when the grandstands around you are filled with those who don't understand what drives you. Champions aren't afraid to take the road less traveled or say no to the unclean food at the king's table.

Champions know that social pressure is not a curse. It's a privilege to endure social pressure on God's center court.

Be His champion. Take chances. Risk obedience. Join up with Him early in the game and shoulder that privilege of pressure. Once you do, His eyes will be planted firmly on you, and His power will be constantly shown on your behalf. Best of all, you'll avoid that haunting, double-minded confusion so often born of compromise in a man's life, especially when it comes to dating and purity.

5

THE DOUBLE MIND

From Fred:

Many young men enter puberty with a resolve to remain a virgin until marriage, but few make the kind of all-out commitment that Jasen made. It's usually the confusion of double-minded thinking that weakens their resolve and stops them short of their goal along the way. That was certainly true in my case.

Sure, you know how my story played out with women. But believe it or not, my commitment to purity was every bit as strong as Jasen's when I entered junior high, and for some very good reasons.

You see, after my parents' divorce, my bedroom was next to Mom's, and on many nights her mournful cries would trickle through the walls. Her heart was broken. She couldn't be the woman Dad wanted—and I'd grow up without a father. Some nights, she'd slip into my room, grab my hands, and desperately search my eyes. "I'm so sorry you don't have your father around here," she'd choke. "And I'm so very sorry I can't be the father you need right now. I'm trying and trying…" I despised my father in those moments, and I swore I'd never treat a woman this way, a vow driven deeply into the bedrock of my soul.

But in seventh grade, I was the star fullback on the Linn-Mar Junior High football team in Marion, Iowa. And as a football player, I got invited to all the best parties, including the one at Kathy Johnson's house one Friday night. Only the most popular kids got invited, so I was definitely feeling like hot stuff.

As a thirteen-year-old, however, I was also pretty nervous. As I entered the house, Kathy's parents welcomed me with open arms, which made me feel a little better. After Mr. Johnson shook my hand, he pointed me toward the stairs leading to the rec room in the basement. "You go have some fun."

I descended the stairs, and when I got to the landing, it was dark. It took my eyes a couple of moments to adjust to the dim light. I was puzzled. *How could they be having any fun with the lights so low?*

I heard some muted voices from the shadows, and then was startled by Janice jumping out in front of me like a big tarantula. All the boys in my class were aware that Janice had blossomed early up top, and as she slyly grinned and brushed against me, my alarms started ringing. Nodding toward the bedroom to her right, she purred, "Wanna play school? I'll be the teacher, and you can be my pet. I'll teach you everything you need to know. Good students really learn a lot in my class."

"Ah, I'm not so sure…"

Janice's face turned to a pout. Over her shoulder, I could barely make out some of my other classmates, who were paired off on the couches. Some of them were making out. I was shocked they'd be kissing in front of everybody. What was up with that?

"Listen, if you try hard in my class, I'll give you an A," Janice continued. "All you have to do is be willing to learn a few things."

Janice wasn't going to give up the chance to school me so easily, and something told me that her first lesson plan would take us well beyond elementary-level kissing. I hadn't even done *that* with a girl before, so I stalled for time. "Uh… uh…I like Amy now," I stammered.

Just then, our host, Kathy, walked up to join our conversation. It was perfect timing for my "teacher."

"Did you hear what Freddie said?" Janice announced to Kathy. "He likes Amy."

The pair looked at each other with Cheshire-cat grins.

"Oh, you *do*," said Kathy. "I think we can do something about that, don't you, Janice?"

With that, the two girls disappeared, and I was grateful not to have to talk to them anymore. I tiptoed past several necking couples, which embarrassed me terribly, and looked for an empty corner where I could pretend to be a lamp and not attract any attention. No such luck. Within a heartbeat, the two girls found me, with Amy locked in their arms between them.

"He didn't get away," Janice said, smacking her gum to appear cool. "Amy, Freddie just told us he likes you."

Oh boy! I wanted to crawl in a hole. I had never even talked to Amy before, and I knew she was way out of my league. In fact, she was out of everyone's league. Amy was the cutest girl at Linn-Mar, and everyone knew it, including this dogface.

"Uh, hi, Amy," I began awkwardly. I tried to come up with something witty to say, but we wimps don't think so fast under the gun. "How are you doing?"

I was the biggest dork this side of the Mississippi.

"I'm fine," Amy said, straightening her shoulders.

An uncomfortable silence fell on the group. Janice and Kathy took this as their cue to exit stage left, smirking the entire time. After they departed, I looked at my feet before saying, "Listen, I'm not—"

"Don't worry about it," Amy replied.

It was getting hot. "I'm going to see if there is anything to eat," I said.

My face burned with embarrassment as I walked up the stairs. After nibbling on some finger foods, I slipped out of Kathy's house that night, feeling demoralized and like an idiot. I didn't like that feeling, and I wondered if I shouldn't get with the program a bit more on this guy/girl thing. I didn't want to look stupid in front of my friends ever again.

As I walked home, my vow to treat girls with respect and tenderness didn't look so important anymore. In subsequent parties, I began to drift from my original, thoughtful stance on how I would treat girls, which goes to show you that one painful social event at Kathy's house was all it took to rock my standards loose. Only one.

The very next time I was alone with a girl, I kissed her, and when she offered me an extra base, I quickly rounded first and slid straight into second. Little by little, girl by girl, I moved further away from my original vow. By the time I reached Stanford several years later, I awoke one morning to a sleepy girl rolling over on my waterbed. Suddenly, a stark wave of revelation slammed me in the head.

I've become my dad!

THE TURN TOWARD SIN

A lot could be said about that slide from Kathy's rec room to my Stanford dorm room, and I've said a lot about it in other books. But there's one critical aspect to the purity process I've never touched on, and it's time I did. Toward that end, take a moment to imagine my painful walk home from Kathy's that night. What really happened inside me as I slipped quietly across the dimly lit streets and cut quickly through the lonely backyard shadows on my way home?

Some might say I took a turn toward sin that night, and there's no question. These moments formed the grinding crucible that crushed my heart and altered the course of my life and relationships for a full decade. But if you take a closer look, what I'd really done that night was turn away from manhood. This is a critically important distinction when it comes to purity. Every man's battle is not so much a fight for your purity as it is a fight for your manhood, a fight for who you are and who you intend to be.

Sexual sin, then, is not your ticket *into* manhood after all—it's your ticket out.

Before that night at Kathy Johnson's party, I was *thinking* like a man. In other words, I was thinking for myself and defending my standards with a single mind. Sure, I was young, but I'd carefully considered how I planned to treat women during my life. My mom's pain had taught me right from wrong, and like any real man, I intended to protect the women around me by living right, no matter what anybody else thought. That's what men do.

On *that* night, however, I let other voices speak up on the matter, and I adjusted my mind accordingly. By the time I got home and flipped on the kitchen lights, I looked a little less like me and a little more like them. I'd stepped toward the group and away from manhood, and I was now thinking with two minds instead of one.

More than thirty-five years later, it's still hard to believe what happened that night. After all, I hated the way my dad used women. Why did I sell out so easily after one measly party?

After all, I know I'm a man, and men shouldn't fall this easily. We're created in God's image, and Exodus 15:3 tells us that "the LORD is a warrior; the LORD is his name." As men, we're created in that image, to fight for great causes and to come through in battle. Why, then, do we buckle under social pressure so quickly?

I've given this question some thought. Oddly enough, it's because we're men. Simon Baron-Cohen's best-selling book *The Essential Difference* explains a key difference between the male and female brains:

> Women tend to value the development of altruistic, reciprocal relation-
> ships. Such relationships require good empathizing skills. In contrast, men
> tend to value power, politics, and competition.... Boys are more likely than
> girls to endorse competitive items...and to rate social status as more impor-
> tant than intimacy.... In a group, boys are quick to establish a "dominance
> hierarchy."... Boys spend more time monitoring and maintaining the hier-
> archy. It seems to matter more to them.... Boys tend to be more often on
> the watch for opportunities to climb socially.
>
> In the summer camp study..., once a boy was put down [verbally]...,
> *other* (lower-status) boys in the cabin jumped in to cement this victim's
> even-lower status. This was a means of establishing their own dominance
> over him.... The male social agenda is more *self-centered* in relation to the
> group, with all the benefits this can bring [like the best invitations and the
> best girls], and it protects one's status within this social system. (brackets
> mine, italics in the original)[1]

This explains a lot, doesn't it? This is why seventh grade is so brutal and why position and rank can dominate your thinking throughout school, even though you're born with a hero's heart. It also helps to explain why a young star fullback at the top of his game would sell out his standards at the first sign of social trouble. My change toward girls had far more to do with my social rank with the guys than it had to do with a desire to kiss a girl.

At Kathy's house, I couldn't have cared less about kissing some girl when the evening began, but as I scurried home that evening, my male brain was screaming, *Listen up! Your place is slipping with the gang!* I did the only sensible thing I could do at the time. I took a slight bow before the great idol, but more ominously, I changed my mind on how I'd be handling women from that day forward. I allowed my peers to define me rather than my own standards on right and wrong. I took on a second mind.

In this sensual culture, our ticket to the top is usually punched by compromise, and because of that, I don't care how strong your beliefs are going in. If you've given the crowd a voice in your thinking, your standards have been watered down, just like mine were. You're no longer single-minded in your approach to girls, or to God, and you probably don't notice it yet.

How do you avoid that? Well, one thing you *can't* do is get rid of your male-style brain, but you *can* redeploy it. Jasen didn't have to dump his brain to opt out on the social rankings at school. He just turned his focus toward a better one—an invisible hierarchy out there in the spiritual realm that rivaled the one at school. Climbing the visible hierarchy brings you favor with the guys around school, but a focus on the invisible one brings you favor and honor with God.

That's the critical message here. Hierarchies themselves are not intrinsically evil. It's the double-mindedness and those ungodly beliefs that you're required to take on to be part of the group that do you in. That's why you must choose to be God's hero as early as possible.

I asked Jasen how he came to think so differently when it came to romantic relationships. He replied, "The crowd won't let me be me, Dad. I'm not going to stand for that. Something deep inside me just says no to all their ways of thinking."

Because the thoughts of the crowd were shut out early in Jasen's life, "being me" and "being Christian" always meant the same thing in his life. He was single-minded in his approach to girls and to life.

That's not true of most of us these days. To keep yourself from slipping with the crowd, you can easily rationalize away your standards, like I did on my way home from Kathy's party. When you do, you end up double-minded in your approach to girls, and "being you" and "being Christian" doesn't mean the same thing for long. When dating, that will be devastating to your purity.

Are you double-minded? You can be pretty certain you are if you're struggling in confusion along these lines: *Why can't I stop this sexual sin with her? After all, I'm a Christian! Why can't I keep my hands off my girlfriend? I should be more spiritual and closer to God.* Even though you've got the mind of Christ and the desire for purity, and even though you've been given everything you need to escape your sexual desires and walk purely with the women in your life (2 Peter 1:3–4), your second, rationalized mind is sabotaging your actions, getting your head—and your hands—moving in the wrong direction whenever you're alone with her.

Clearly, opting out on popularity would have been extremely helpful to me in my battle for purity, just like it was for Jasen. Avoiding folks like Kathy and Janice would have gone a long way in helping me keep my original vows and beliefs intact, no doubt about it.

Still, that alone wouldn't have been enough to keep the double-minded thinking out of my life completely, and it wouldn't have been enough in Jasen's life, either, for that matter. You see, there's a second voice out there calling out that second mind in you. Sure, the voice of your peers is plenty loud, but so is the voice of the media. That means there is one more early decision you must make regarding the media if you're to keep your thinking straight with the girls, as this next story illustrates.

SHOWN THE DOOR

Lindsey was one of the smart girls. Sitting in many of my college prep classes, she wasn't the most beautiful girl there, but she was definitely cute, and so incredibly nice. She wore a cross necklace to school every day. I don't know why, but that attracted me, and while she wasn't the most popular girl on campus, her sweetness and purity tugged at my heart. With the football season long over and snow still covering the baseball diamonds, I had some time on my hands, so I somehow mustered the courage to ask her out.

I can't remember what we did, but we ended up at her house and, at some point, we began to kiss. I found it all very exciting, and she seemed to like it too. Problem was, I didn't stop there. Before long, I found my hands roaming.

Suddenly, like a threatened lioness, Lindsey pushed me away, stood up, and began roaring. "Who do you think you are to touch me like this? You are just like all the other guys! All you care about is getting some action, you pig! You don't care about me at all."

That's the condensed version, at least. Like a beaten puppy, I slunk outside to the car. I was ashamed, but I wasn't completely sure why. Mostly, I was shocked. Here was this girl I liked and respected so much and who I wouldn't hurt for the world, and yet I had just been given the boot out of her house, dragging my tail to my car in confusion. *What did I do?*

All I knew was what I *hadn't* done. You see, I wasn't out to "get some," as she accused me. I was simply showing my affection for her, believing that getting physical was the way you do that if your intentions are serious. Because of my parents' divorce, my only teachers were Hollywood and locker rooms, so what else would I think? Twisted as it may seem, I genuinely thought I *was* showing her she was different and special, and that I *did* care.

Again, this story is one more example of why you need to be careful what you watch, and why the teen years are not throwaway years. You cannot afford to take the socially easy way out on movies if you are a young man. This is the time for building up your heroic heart so you can make those tough, early decisions that establish exactly who you are as a man.

Again, it's not just that voice of the crowd that delivers double-minded thinking. Lining up your life with TV, movies, and music can also do it. It certainly did it to me. Because my first mind had vowed to treat women with respect, I genuinely thought I *was* different from all the other guys, but I was mistaken. My second mind had picked up some disrespectful ideas from Hollywood about the way women and relationships worked, and I hadn't a clue it had even happened until my hands went too far with poor Lindsey.

Eventually, all those films and the shower-room fables stole my manhood right out from under me—and I was clueless about that too, until my best college friend connected the dots for me.

Right around the time I had that "I've become my dad" revelation at Stanford, a lovely girl had broken up with Bryan. I knew he was still hoping to get back together with her. But despite that, after waiting a respectful amount of time, I asked if he'd mind if I took her out. "Sure, go ahead," he said, so I jumped at the chance, and before long things had once again spun out of control and we ended up sleeping together. It didn't take long for the news to reach Bryan, and he was furious. In his mind, his hopes of reestablishing their relationship were now trashed.

He stormed to my room and launched a vicious verbal barrage at me. Just as the bombardment was ending, his eyes flashed once more. "All you ever think about is yourself!" he shouted. "When it comes to women, all your brains are in your pants!"

I was stricken deeply. I knew I'd hurt him, and harsh words from a friend naturally hound anyone for days, even weeks. But when his words kept troubling me mercilessly for months, I knew this was more than an emotional bruise on me. He had scratched something disturbing, deep in my heart.

Simply said, I was no longer a man. I was a slave to my sexual satisfaction. When it came to girls and my sexuality, a second set of brains really were in my pants. Nothing about me was heroic, and no woman could count on me at all. When it came to our purity together, I'd lost every man's battle.

The reason God calls us away from sexual sin is because it destroys everything in its path. I was living proof. My strength was gone, and so was my resolve as a man. If your ears are still hanging on the voice of the crowd and your eyes are as hooked on Hollywood as ever, it's very likely that you, too, have picked up a second way of thinking toward girls and dating. If you don't watch your step, your manhood will be drained faster than an oil change at a Jiffy Lube.

THE FACEBOOK TEST

If you're anything like I was, of course, you haven't yet noticed how double-minded you are, or how much of your manhood has been stolen by these social ladders and the media. But you needn't worry, because some genuine insight may be as near as your Facebook profile. What does your profile reveal about you?

Perhaps I can connect a few dots for you, just as my friend Bryan once did for me at Stanford. See if you can spot anything amiss in this combined profile of three pastors' sons who say they want to get into the ministry. While I won't share their names, all of them claim the Bible among their favorite books, with *How to Hear from God*, *Wild at Heart*, and *Every Young Man's Battle* among the others. Main interests include "my life with God" and "following Jesus Christ." Favorite music? "All forms of music sung to my Father."

Wow. How bold! As soldiers in God's kingdom, they must surely be in Special Ops, right? You might think so until you take a look at some of their favorite movies: *Lucky Number Slevin*, *Thank You for Smoking*, *Wedding Crashers*, *Fever Pitch*, *Out Cold*, *Garden State*, *Almost Famous*, *The 40-Year-Old Virgin*, *Knocked Up*, *Man on Fire*, *Anchorman: The Legend of Ron Burgundy*, *The Departed*, and *Moulin Rouge!*—all rated PG-13 and R for sex or nudity.

I've not viewed these movies myself, but thanks to ScreenIt.com, I can tell you that in these films you'll find any sort of sexual depravity you can imagine. But before we move forward, I want to warn you that there are two paragraphs below that may be difficult for some of you to read. I am not trying to be salacious, and I am not pandering shock value. In fact, I'd prefer not to include these descriptions at all.

But I've got a problem. As I've crisscrossed this hemisphere challenging guys to consider cleaning up their entertainment, I've found that the desensitizing effect of the sensuality in these films has so warped their conscience, they no longer even notice when it passes before their eyes. In other words, they can actually watch films like those listed above and deem them "pretty clean." If I don't "name names" on these films and point out the problems in black and white, many of you won't understand what I'm saying. And since it's critical that you do understand, I have no choice but to include these two paragraphs below.

So, here goes.

Pop those DVDs into your player and these scenes will pass before you: crude depictions of male and female masturbation; intercourse; oral sex; lewd gags about each of these supposedly casual and common acts; obscene double entendres about sex organs and borrowing sugar; countless closeups of crotches; provocative bordello dancing; filthy double entendres from a woman hungrily begging a man for sex; crass references to the seductive power of weddings and funerals; nymphomania, both spoken of and depicted; innumerable suggestive images of every body part imaginable; a girl fondling a man beneath the table at her parents' formal dinner party; a barely covered woman riding a slow-bucking mechanical bull in a highly sexualized way at a rowdy public bar; all manner of bare skin and body parts; coarse come-ons; perverse hookups; vile jokes about the arousing nature of lesbian encounters; crude quips about sodomy, bestiality, pedophilia, and necrophilia; sordid sex jokes about Jesus and His mother, Mary; and more tasteless references and inventive slang phrases than I have time to mention relating sex to sports, politics, business, space exploration, road construction, drug use, music, high school, and many other common interests, occupations, and pursuits.

You'll catch vivid scenes of rear-entry intercourse, and see a girl straddling some guy while reaching for his crotch and lewdly joking that she's not wearing any underwear. You'll be there when a girlfriend finds her boyfriend making out with another girl, wearing only panties and bra, and then you'll stumble across some extremely sensual games of Spin the Bottle and spot some students paying bellhops to let them peek through holes to watch people having sex. You'll also hear some mournful guy lamenting that if he could only have sex with the girl that rejected him in high school, he could exorcise all his demons. You'll later bump into a woman declaring that sex is a basic human right and that no girl should ever let her boyfriend come between her and a quickie with an acquaintance.

These movies are odd entertainment for any Christian young man, let alone pastoral students who claim that their main focus in life is God. These guys are still stuck in a self-serving, selfish phase regarding their sexuality and their choices of sexualized media and movies—and they don't even recognize it. See how easy it is for a guy's manhood to be stolen right out from under his nose? These guys are part of the church's next generation of leaders, and yet they're watching, and laughing merrily at, perversions that would make any real man turn away and blush.

What does your Facebook profile reveal about you? We're seeing an epidemic of double-mindedness in our culture today. These three young men can't even tell right from wrong anymore, and it's clear that being a pastoral student doesn't necessarily mean being a man of God anymore.

For too long, we've accepted such double-minded thinking, brushing it off as no big deal, expecting grace and "being relevant" to cover it. But how can these future pastors lead anyone anywhere but into their own compromised pit? God has this to say to these prospective shepherds:

"They dress the wound of my people as though it were not serious. 'Peace, peace,' they say, when there is no peace. Are they ashamed of their loathsome conduct? No, they have no shame at all; they do not even know how to blush. So they will fall among the fallen; they will be brought down when I punish them," says the LORD.

This is what the LORD says: "Stand at the crossroads and look; ask for the ancient paths, ask where the good way is, and walk in it, and you will find rest for your souls. But you said, 'We will not walk in it.'" (Jeremiah 6:14–16)

If you've been accepting this kind of entertainment, maybe you've become blind as well:

Go to this people and say, "You will be ever hearing but never understanding; you will be ever seeing but never perceiving." For this people's heart has become calloused; they hardly hear with their ears, and they have closed their eyes. Otherwise they might see with their eyes, hear with their ears, understand with their hearts and turn, and I would heal them. (Acts 28:26–27)

Since our attitudes are no different today than they were in the days of Jeremiah and Paul, these warnings are ours to be heeded too, as well as this one: If you can take in the base immorality of *Wedding Crashers* right on through to the final credits without turning it off, you are sexually perverted. Your mind has been split into two, and you're nowhere near living the hero's life to which God has called you. What's more, your chances of staying pure with a girlfriend are bleak at best.

First of all, when it comes to dating, the heavy sensuality of these films alone will compromise your defenses severely:

Such sensuous [films] can sumo-size a sex drive faster than you can say, "I'll make mine supersize." If you can't control your sex drive, whose fault is it? Is it God's, for giving you the sex drive? Or is it yours, because you've jumped on the gas pedal and sped past the red line far too often?

You've got a decision to make. You can't visually feed on the same films as your school chums and expect to stay sexually pure.[2]

The visuals are dangerous enough, all right, but in the context of dating, the even *greater* danger is that you're likely to pick up some warped strongholds of thinking about romantic relationships from these films without even knowing it, much like the one that bubbled out of control on my date with Lindsey and got my hands roaming to "show her I cared." What are "strongholds of thought"? They're sympathetic attitudes toward sin in your life, the building blocks of double-minded thinking. These strongholds give Satan his footholds of authority in your life. And if you have been freely partaking of today's media, you'll have more of these to deal with in life. One obvious example of a sympathetic attitude toward sin would be this one: *I have freedom in Christ to watch anything I want to because God knows my heart and because His grace covers all.*

What a treacherous trap! That lie might be true if grace erased both the sin *and* its consequences, but it doesn't. Worst of all, if you believe that lie, the corrupt films you've been watching have established *other* dangerous enemy strongholds of thought in your life about girls and relationships. These double-minded thought patterns will eventually drop your defenses when you are alone with a girl, no matter how desperately you want to stay pure with her in your heart.

Consider a few examples of the lies you can pick up from your compromised entertainment:

- If you aren't kissing, you aren't really dating.
- If you don't date a lot, you won't know what you want in a wife.
- We need to express our sexuality, whether married or not. We're wired that way.
- I need sexual experience now, or I'll embarrass myself on my wedding night.
- There are two kinds of girls: the kind you date and the kind you marry.
- Premarital sex doesn't hurt her any more than it hurts me.
- When it comes to sex, women are like guys—they want it too.
- You need to know if you're sexually compatible before marriage.
- Knowing her sexually is the fastest way to get to know her personally.

If you currently believe some of these, stop and ask yourself, *Who taught me these things?* Your teachers were either that carnal crowd at school or some corrupt cache of movies, and as long as these strongholds remain standing in your life, your purity with your girlfriend will be compromised, because they will drop your defenses somewhere along the way.

How do these strongholds drop your defenses? Take that last statement from the list above, for example: *Knowing her sexually is the fastest way to get to know her personally.* When the going gets hot and the passion is boiling, you're already sympathetic to this lie that the enemy begins whispering from the heart of that stronghold, and soon you're rationalizing, *Hey, it's really not so bad if we go too far sexually tonight. After all, getting to know her sexually is the fastest way to get to know her personally, so it won't be a total loss even if I do let the defenses slip a little bit. We can't help but learn something important about ourselves as a couple.* How can sex be all that bad if it performs such a useful service for your relationship, right?

That's how the double-minded guy thinks, and that's why so many "reputable" and "trustworthy" Christian men end up pushing girls over the edge sexually. These double-minded lies destroy your resolve as a man, and they will eventually destroy your romantic relationships, over and over again. The films you choose to watch *do* matter, no matter how deep your pool of grace.

Listen. I'm not trying to come down hard against all movies. I've got an enormous collection of DVDs—hundreds of titles old and new. You don't have to stop watching movies altogether. You've simply got to take charge of your destiny as a man and take control of your viewing habits. Quit letting the crowd define what you watch. My rule of thumb is: if it pollutes, it's out of bounds.

Obviously, the heavy visual sensuality pollutes, but there's also a broader, more subtle dimension to this pollution that you should notice as well. You see, the characters and attitudes depicted in those movies from the Facebook profiles I mentioned earlier exist *only* in the dark corners of a twisted mind's wishful thinking. Think about it. In all my running around after women, you'd think I'd have seen at least some women like the sex-obsessed girls depicted in these films. But strangely, I never did. That's because, for the most part, they are fantasy, existing only in the dark places of someone's mind.

The trouble is, when you watch this pollution over and over, those fantasies warp into some very real strongholds of thinking in your mind. That's how I came to believe that it was normal to go too far physically with Lindsey on our first date, for instance. That's also how I came to believe that if I wasn't kissing, I wasn't dating, and that I could never really get to know a girl deeply without having sex with her.

When it comes to defending your purity on a date, that kind of mental pollution is even more dangerous than the heavy sensuality in these films, because you don't even know it's there. If you are going to take charge of your destiny as a man and your purity with your girlfriends, you need to take control of your viewing habits and keep the lies and fantasies at bay in your life. You need to quit warping your view of women and relationships, and you need to tear down those strongholds of thought and dump that second mind from your life.

Jasen learned to take responsibility for his entertainment early on, and that's why he began stepping out of his junior high classrooms on his own. That kept the visual sensuality out of his life and kept him from sumo-sizing his sex drive. But even more important for his dating relationships, it kept the double-minded thinking out of his life. That's so important.

Again, think about it. Jasen and I both began our teens with a deep commitment to respect the women in our lives sexually, but we ended up miles apart. I wanted to be popular, and I didn't take charge of my media choices, so I rationalized things and developed a double mind when it came to women. Jasen *did* opt out on popularity and *did* take charge of his media choices, so he believed none of the stronghold lies that were so common in my way of thinking. That's why he left every girl better off for having known him, and I left none of them that way.

That's so critical to remember. When it comes to sexual purity with girls, it'll be the lies that you believe about romantic relationships that will do you in most of the time. If you want to get your purity on track, you need to rip those lies out of your life: "We demolish arguments and every pretension that sets itself up against the knowledge of God, and we take captive every thought to make it obedient to Christ" (2 Corinthians 10:5).

It's time to man up, my friend. Shoot the traitors and retrain your mind. "Do not conform any longer to the pattern of this world, but be transformed by the renewing of your mind" (Romans 12:2).

From my perspective as Jasen's father, the most unique thing about him from his earliest days of puberty was his choice to reject the polluting influences of popularity and entertainment. Those traitorous strongholds of thought never made it into his mind, so God's truths always had their full sway in his life. Over the years, I believe that was the single greatest factor that kept him from tripping up with the girls.

Maybe you haven't made the decisions Jasen did. Maybe these strongholds have you bound up, and you just can't keep your hands to yourself. Well, don't worry, my friend. I was in the same place. Those strongholds can still come tumbling down, as they did for me.

During my first year as a Christian back in Iowa, a young woman lived upstairs in my apartment complex. She was having trouble with her boyfriend and feeling lonely, so she'd come down to my apartment to talk and watch TV three or four nights a week.

She was incredibly attractive to me, and many times, she'd cuddle up next to me, often crying as she poured out her heart. I knew exactly what to do to seduce her. She was emotionally vulnerable, and I was being sensitive and thoughtful in our discussions, which every woman loves in a man. We were all alone, and all I had to do was push a couple key buttons and she would be mine.

But this time around, I didn't do it. I didn't kiss her, and I never touched her with dishonor, nothing. Granted, it wasn't exactly wise to be alone with her in my apartment, but I did stand. As time passed, she recovered emotionally, and eventually her boyfriend asked to get back together. Today, they've been married for over twenty-five years, and I'm so grateful I chose to protect her in her time of weakness.

That, of course, brings us back around full circle to the vows of a young man listening to his mother's mournful cries through the walls of his bedroom. After all those wasted years, I'd finally begun tearing down those strongholds of thought in my life. I was finally becoming all I'd once promised to be around women. And today, God has finished what He began in me back then, and I am all He intended me to be as a man.

It's never too late to demolish *your* strongholds, my friend. You just have to know where they are in your thinking. Toward that end, Jasen and I (with some help from Rose) will take on the nine most common lies one by one over the next nine chapters, using God's truth and our own stories to bring them out into the open so that you finish this demolition job in your life.

You, too, can be victorious. It's time to risk obedience, and it's time to reduce these strongholds to ruins.

You already have the weapons and the divine power to get the job done.

Now it's time to get started.

6

THE PROMISE OF PAIN

Stronghold Myth #1: I was born sexual, and I have to express that, whether single or not. I'm just wired that way, and it's unfair for God to ask otherwise.

I met Alex one morning at a small retreat center in central Iowa after speaking to a large group of men from one of Iowa State's campus ministries. He'd been hanging back and waiting for the others to have their turns to speak with me. When the coast was clear, Alex finally stepped up.

"I've thought about this sexual purity thing from top to bottom. I'm absolutely certain that since God gave me a sexual side, it only makes sense that He's provided a pure form of sexual release outside of marriage. Can you please tell me what that might be?"

Alex had a serious stronghold of thought. As a reminder, strongholds are sympathetic attitudes toward sin, or buying in to the wisdom of this world by lining up our minds with our schools, media, and culture. Whether he knew it or not, Alex had lined up with this one: *I was born sexual, and so I have to express it. I'm wired that way.*

Where did he pick up that mind-set? Certainly not from God, as Christ was crucified so that we might think otherwise: "For the grace of God that brings salvation has appeared to all men. It teaches us to say 'No' to ungodliness and worldly passions, and to live self-controlled, upright and godly lives in this present age" (Titus 2:11–12).

Alex seemed frustrated and just couldn't believe the position that God had placed him in as a single guy on the sensual Iowa State campus. After talking things over for a while, Alex thanked me for my time and sauntered off to meet his girlfriend in the cafeteria. As I gathered up my briefcase and books to haul them out to the car, my thoughts returned to an entry I'd read on one of Iowa State's message boards after I spoke to a thousand students about purity on the Cyclone campus. One in particular stood out to me: "What's this Fred guy talking about? We are animals. We're wired for sex, and it's as natural as belching. We might as well enjoy it with everyone we can."

We *do* have good wiring, no doubt about it. In fact, few animals enjoy sex as much as we do. But while good wiring makes for good sex, it doesn't necessarily make sex good—or good for us—outside of marriage.

And it certainly doesn't mean that we should change God's standard of purity to accommodate our wiring.

This sympathetic attitude has even wormed its way into the church. I've spoken often about purity in singles groups, and it wasn't long before I heard comments like, *So I'm not supposed to have even a hint of sexual immorality in my life? Come on, God loves us! He couldn't possibly have meant what He said in Ephesians 5:3. He knows we don't get married as early in life as they did in Bible times, so those commands to hold off on sex until marriage are completely outdated.*

Hmm. Do we really think God is sitting in heaven, blushing and shaking his head in embarrassment while opining, *Oh boy, this one really caught me off guard, Gabriel. How was I supposed to know there would be a bigger gap between puberty and marriage in the twenty-first century? I sure wish I could erase that part in Ephesians where I told them to avoid every hint of sexuality in their lives, but it's too late now. I guess I'll just have to hope the enlightened ones will ignore Me!*

This is a warped way of thinking that takes our eyes completely off the point. As I packed my books into my car, I marveled once more at my son Jasen. He was a real man to be reckoned with spiritually, and he'd grown willing to suffer almost anything to protect his sexual purity. Jasen was single, wired for sex, and living in the same sensual college environment as Alex, yet nothing about God's call to purity seemed particularly unfair to him. Unlike Alex, he always had a peaceful bearing and lack of confusion while discussing the general battle for sexual purity with me, and he'd obviously evaded the stronghold myth that opened this chapter.

I mused that Jasen was winning *his* battle because he saw the bigger picture in his fight for purity. Guys who focus on the "unfairness" of being single with a sex drive usually end up on a manic search for an easy way out, but not Jasen. He was settled because he understood that the battle for purity was about far more than simply trying to keep your hands clean and your eyes and heart pure. It was really a battle for his manhood, the highest stakes possible, and that changed the entire game for him.

You don't engage this battle just to become clean. You do it to become *you*, and all you were meant to be as a man.

As I pulled out of the campus that day, it suddenly hit me: *Sex is not a guy's ticket into manhood. Suffering is.*

Many Christians believe that God never intended for His children to suffer, but I don't believe that's true. Think about it. Do you believe God regrets the suffering Jasen endured as he wrestled with his will during those lonely days at the beginning of middle school? Not on your life. In fact, when the Lord saw Jasen's willingness to opt out of the social ladders for the sake of God's purposes, I think the Lord's heart was jumping! *All right! My boy Jasen is getting somewhere!*

Such suffering has always been a guy's ticket into manhood from the day Adam took his first breath amidst Eden's splendor. If you're thinking there wasn't any suffering in the Garden of Eden, you'd be mistaken. Remember how God planted the Tree of the Knowledge of Good and Evil smack in the middle of the lush garden? God didn't place that tree in the far corner where Adam wouldn't see it every day, nor did he surround the Tree of Knowledge with fencing topped with razor wire.

Instead, God set that beautiful tree with tantalizing fruit right in front of Adam's nose as a challenge to his will, knowing that His command *not* to eat the fruit would eventually move Adam from being a man of great potential to one of full maturity…if he made the right choice each day. That choice was vivid and stark: Adam had to deny his immediate desires for the sake of God's promise of greater fulfillment in the future.

Even though everything was perfect in the garden, Adam had to obey this one command from God: he couldn't eat the fruit, or he would surely die. God confronted Adam's will this way to draw out his character, to help him become all he could be. Adam would grow as he grappled daily with the Lord's question: *Will you choose Me over your own desires?*

This kind of suffering was planned into men's lives by God from the beginning. The confrontation of the will—and the suffering your flesh endures as you wrestle to make the right choices day after day—is the developmental tool that the Father uses to bring every son into manhood, and it's also the way you enter into a deeper intimacy with God that you didn't have before. Your trust grows deeper, and that's when settled peace infuses your life, like the peace I saw in Jasen.

He even put His only Son, Jesus, through this process:

> During the days of Jesus' life on earth, he offered up prayers and petitions
> with loud cries and tears to the one who could save him from death, and
> he was heard because of his reverent submission. Although he was a son, *he
> learned obedience from what he suffered* and, once made perfect, he became
> the source of eternal salvation for all who obey him and was designated by
> God to be high priest in the order of Melchizedek. (Hebrews 5:7–10)

> In bringing many sons to glory, it was fitting that God…should make the
> author of their salvation perfect through suffering. (Hebrews 2:10)

Now, let's be clear about these two scriptures. When it says that Jesus was made perfect through suffering, we're not talking about moral purity or innocence. Jesus was innocent from birth. He never sinned, and He was never morally defiled.

Still, God's plan for Jesus was the same one He had for an innocent Adam back in the garden: to take that wonderful, sinless human potential and, through the confrontation of His will, grow His manhood into its full potential as a mature, holy man of character. Jesus, the last Adam (1 Corinthians 15:45), finished the path that our first Adam could only begin.

In the end, Adam didn't deny himself when offered a bite of Eve's apple. Jesus denied Himself all the way to the cross.

From Jasen:

There's a lot to learn from Adam because there's a lot we can relate to in his story. Think about it. During your development years in high school and college, you sit in a garden paradise much like Eden. Late adolescence and the young adult years are often seen as an extended break between childhood and the "real life" that comes after college, and most of your needs during that time are met by others. The culture expects you to produce very little of value socially and economically during this time. In *your* Eden, little is even expected of you morally, and most slide down to meet those expectations without realizing what it costs them in their development as men.

In short, there's little out there to confront our wills. We know that Adam had his tree in the garden, but what is *our* tree in *our* paradise? What is that grinding crucible through which our wills must pass?

Don't look now, but it's your sexuality. It's sitting there beautifully in the center of your garden, confronting your will, tugging and pulling at your eyes and your heart, day in and day out. The Tree of Sexuality, as it were, is situated in the perfect place to help you grow while you suffer and grapple daily with this all-important question: will you choose God over your sexual desires?

No way! That wouldn't be fair of God. Besides, the entire world knows abstinence is a relic and completely impossible. Times have changed. God isn't ignorant of that.

Maybe. But what if popular culture is wrong, and God knows exactly what He's doing?

I often hear guys say, "God wouldn't have made women beautiful if He didn't want us to look at them." But how could God confront your will if women *weren't* beautiful?

I've also heard guys argue, "God wouldn't have given us such a strong sex drive with no way to quench it."

Oh, really? How can we be sure about that? Well, the quickest way to judge whether a man's position is accurate is to take a peek at his underlying assumptions. What assumption is asserted here?

A kind God would never ask His children to wrestle with frustration or deny themselves.

Sorry to be the bearer of bad news, but that's a bogus assumption and completely unbiblical. A kind God *must* ask us to struggle or He isn't kind at all. There is no other way for you to grow in God, and there are no easy steps into manhood.

Besides, in our world, what else could confront our wills so effectively? Nearly everything else is ready-made and immediately available to us, and even our Christian lives demand little of us. (Try living in Iran or China as a Christian!) Perhaps your campus ministry asks you to volunteer to clean up the football stadium after home games as a service to God. Perhaps you go on a mission trip every year or so (usually paid for by the donations of others). These are worthwhile projects, to be sure, but they don't demand much of you. And they certainly don't require Olympian effort or a single-minded commitment in the face of intense enemy fire, at least not the kind the apostle Paul spoke of:

> Do you not know that in a race all the runners run, but only one gets the
> prize? Run in such a way as to get the prize. Everyone who competes in the
> games goes into strict training. They do it to get a crown that will not last;
> but we do it to get a crown that will last forever. Therefore I do not run
> like a man running aimlessly; I do not fight like a man beating the air. No,
> I beat my body and make it my slave so that after I have preached to

others, I myself will not be disqualified for the prize. (1 Corinthians 9:24–27)

What Paul had in mind is the kind of confrontation that'll put hair on a man's chest. You need this kind of grinding confrontation of your will to shape your manhood. Where is that kind of suffering going to come from in life?

It'll come through your sexuality, especially during your single years. In spite of the long, difficult wait between puberty and marriage, male sexuality is not a curse. It's a blessing, that we might become complete in Him.

But that's unfair for God to use my sexuality that way!

Is it unfair, or is it just hard? Is it mean spirited, or is it a loving ticket into manhood? Is it an impossible task, or are you just unwilling to pay the price of purity?

From Fred:

If it seems unfair, then what do you do with Jasen, who never once thought the cards he was dealt were unfair? What do you do with all the other guys who simply shouldered their weapons and turned their hearts toward God until their right choices became habits?

Zachary tells us how he made the right choices his habits:

I have been assailed by sexual sin ever since puberty, but now I'm using the tools you taught me in *Every Young Man's Battle.* I've come up with another tool that has been very useful in my own war against sexual sin, and maybe it can help others. When my mind is hit by temptation, I escape by simply bombarding my mind with tons of different thoughts until I simply forget about the original temptation. For instance, if I feel a strong urge to bring up some porn, I drop a sort of cluster bomb and begin to think of other things in a string, along these lines:

- What are all the major assault rifles of the world and their caliber?
- What is my grandmother's maiden name, and how many letters are in it?
- What is the definition of the word *word*?
- What are the reasons I don't want to participate in the sport of skateboarding?
- What's up with that whole interpretive dance thing anyway?

This is particularly useful since guys tend to be able to only focus on one thing at a time and also have the habit of moving quickly from one thing to another. I have found that I often forget I was being tempted and continue with my day after doing this. My dad used this same process when he quit smoking cold turkey years ago. He would just focus on a hubcap of a moving car or watch one blade of a ceiling fan, forgetting the temptation for a minute or two until his cravings passed a little.

I had all but given up hope of beating sexual sin, and like so many others, I'd given up on getting free until I got married. But after reading your book, I suspected that was a lie, and I didn't think marriage would make the fight any more easy than it was right now. I had to just get up and get it done. I am getting better now, and I feel cleaner and closer to God than I have in a long time.

Zachary stopped seeing his sexuality as a curse, and the discipline he's now learned will help him grow into the hero he was always meant to be. He's become more than he could have ever been otherwise.

Not only that, I have this sneaking suspicion that God is bragging about guys like Jasen and Zachary, just like He bragged about Job: "Have you considered my servant Job? There is no one on earth like him; he is blameless and upright, a man who fears God and shuns evil" (Job 1:8).

God could be telling everyone, *Hey, did you see what My boy Jasen did? He opted out on popularity for Me, and now look at him! He's grown up, and he's fulfilling every dream I had for him. And how about Zachary? He may have started out slow, but once he found out how to distract his mind, he started blossoming. There aren't many like him yet, but he's setting a great example. There will be more like him soon.*

When God asks you to avoid eating the fruit from the Tree of Sexuality, He's confronting your will. You already know His will, and you also know that He's given you everything you need to walk in the divine nature, like keeping your eyes pure, taming your sexual passions while you're single, and making every girl better off for having known you. You have all the potential in the world because you have all the grace in the world at your disposal.

When you deny your flesh, you *do* experience temporary pain, but the strength you gain provides a strong conviction that God is always good, and that He's not playing games with your sexuality. He hasn't stirred up desires only to tease you. Instead, you eventually find that He always fulfills you if you walk in His ways sexually, and He always satisfies the longings of your heart.

In short, this stronghold—*I'm sexual, so I have to express it*—must go. When the going gets hot and heavy with your girl, you'll give in to this lie out of pity for yourself. Why not take on a sympathetic attitude toward God's wisdom, instead of pitying yourself and lining up with the wisdom of the world? Heroism and manhood are your birthrights as a man of God, just like they were for Adam. Sure, Adam failed by choosing his desires over God's, just as we often choose our girlfriends—and their bodies—over the Lord. But we don't have to do that.

In fact, we can't *afford* to do that anymore. We need to step up. The damage to our culture caused by Christian men waiting too long to step into manhood has been devastating. Your years as a single man are not throwaway years, and your sexuality is not some unfair curse on your life. It's time to tear down that stronghold of thought, and it's also time for a countercultural rebellion against the spirit of Baal so that we might stop the physical and emotional damage we now have cascading over our girls.

FAILING HER

> **Stronghold Myth #2:** When it comes to sex, women are like guys—they want it too. Besides, premarital sex doesn't hurt her any more than it hurts me.

Look again at this familiar myth. Who taught you this? The guys in the locker room? *Sex and the City* reruns?

It certainly wasn't the Bible. The Word asserts that there are considerable differences between men and women, and you are to lead accordingly in your dating relationships. If you don't take these differences into account, it'll hinder your communication and your relationship with God: "Husbands, in the same way be considerate as you live with your wives, and treat them with respect *as the weaker partner* and as heirs with you of the gracious gift of life, so that nothing will hinder your prayers" (1 Peter 3:7).

In the original Greek language, the term for "weaker partner" can also be translated "fine china," which I think is a better translation in this context. How do you handle fine china? With respect, as you tenderly appreciate and display its finest points. You don't slam fine china around or put it through the blast of the dishwasher.

We haven't listened very well. We treat our girls like tin plates in a campground, trampling their femininity and their souls. Here's what some young women have told me about the guys in their lives:

- My boyfriend recently told me that he has been having struggles with porn. I had a hard time hearing this, especially because we have been dating for a year and a half, and all I have known from him has been his high moral standards. The one question I have is this: how do I learn how to respect men the same way I used to? I have a hard time looking at him and not thinking, "I wonder what sin he has gotten himself into." So why are men so sick?

- I feel like women are nothing more than sex objects to guys, and all they want to do is jump us. When I think about past relationships I've had, I see that I was always the one stopping them from going too far. If I hadn't slammed the brakes, they would have gladly gone farther. I get so ticked off when they treat me like a piece of meat, like whistling at me or looking me up and down. I feel like I have to wear a thick snowsuit all the time so I'll be sure not to turn on any guys.

- I just got married to my college boyfriend, and I've just found out he's been cheating on me with pornography. My self-esteem is crushed. We are in counseling, hoping to reconnect as husband and wife, but I cannot even think of doing so now because I feel so ugly and disgusting. I cannot even change my clothes in the same room since I can't get the images of what I have seen on his computer out of my mind.

Women learn to resent men early on, and rightly so. They feel unprotected, and that's our fault, not theirs. When the carnage from the spirit of Baal hit us, we didn't stand up and stop it, so now our wives and girlfriends are reaping the whirlwind with us.

My own daughter Laura senses it too. As she stood proudly in her purple cap and gown with her classmates at high school graduation, giggling and sharing their hopes and dreams, one of the star running backs had his future all mapped out. "I'm heading to college with one goal in mind," he said. "I'm going to lay as many women as possible, and then I'm going to find a pure one to settle down with to raise a family."

Four years later, Laura and I were sitting at Starbucks together, discussing her impending move to North Carolina State for grad school. "Daddy, I know you tell me that there are godly men out there looking for a girl like me, and I want to believe you," she said. "But in all my years of church, youth group, and campus ministries, I've never met a single guy who's all that concerned about his sexual purity."

That comment should make us quake in our boots. I don't believe Laura is alone in her near despair over the situation we've created as men. What have we done? How can our relationships with women thrive in the shadow of such rampant darkness? Women need men to be fiercely devoted to the truth and to purity, and fiercely devoted to protecting their women's hearts and souls. Where will they find such men?

Our girlfriends and our wives are masterpieces of God's finest china, lovely in His sight. Every woman you ever encounter is a daughter of the King and is to be protected and guarded and treated with the utmost dignity and respect. What does it say about you if you abuse them with your hands, your eyes, or your heart? You're no hero, that's for sure. Remember, you're called to protect them, and for good reason. Men and women are fundamentally different in the way they approach intimate relationships.

Miriam Grossman, author of *Unprotected*, is an MD at a counseling center at one of our nation's best-known universities. You won't hear this on the news, but she says her office is packed with bright, accomplished young women looking for relief from crying jags, sleepless nights, relentless worrying, and thoughts of death.

When she tells the story of Olivia, an eighteen-year-old freshman who was valedictorian of her high school class and planning for med school, you can't help but see the Lord's "fine china" being destroyed all around us.

Dr. Grossman writes that Olivia was certainly an accomplished student, but she had been bulimic in the past, sometimes vomiting six times a day from emotional distress. She'd first developed bulimia in the ninth grade, but she'd done so well with therapy that the bouts of binging and vomiting disappeared—until she landed in college.

The academic pressures weren't the problem. It was her dating life causing this deep, soul-level distress. The end of a romance triggered a relapse, and this is how

Olivia described her short-lived relationship, which included her first sexual experience:

> "When it ended, it hurt so much," she said, weeping. "I think about
> him all the time, and I haven't been going to one of my classes, because
> he'll be there, and I can't handle seeing him. I was so unprepared for
> this.... Why, Doctor," she asked, "why do they tell you how to protect
> your body—from herpes and pregnancy—but they don't tell you what
> it does to your *heart*?"
>   Olivia was a smart girl asking a good question. Why are students
> inundated with information about contraception, a healthy diet, sleep
> hygiene, coping with stress and pressure—but not a word about the havoc
> that casual sex plays on young women's emotions? It's not as if there isn't
> any research on the subject. (italics in the original)[1]

Dr. Grossman is right. Check the research. Do girls handle broken relationships as well as guys do?

Not even close.

In one recent study of 6,500 adolescents, sexually active teenage girls were found to be at least three times more likely to be depressed than the girls who were not sexually active.[2] In another study of 8,000 teens, two researchers concluded that "females experience a larger increase in depression than males in response to romantic involvement" and "females' greater vulnerability to romantic involvement may explain the higher rates of depression in female teens."[3]

In other words, Olivia was hurt far more than the guy who dumped her, and Dr. Grossman's assessment was absolutely shocking:

> I've seen so many students like these, they blur together in my mind, a
> pitiable crowd of confused, vulnerable young women, ill prepared for
> campus life, making poor choices, and paying high prices.
>   No amount of Prozac or Zoloft is going to solve this problem. These

young women must, for their physical and emotional well-being, change their lifestyle.... Is it feasible? To acknowledge the negative consequences of the anything-goes, hooking-up culture would challenge the notion that women are just like men.[4]

As much as you've been taught to believe that men and women are alike in every fundamental way, I hope you realize just how bogus that notion is. Women aren't like men. Men aren't like women. And not only does the Bible tell us that, but modern science has proven it time and again.

In this case, significant brain differences between men and women play a huge role in our differing responses to relationship pain. We have two types of brains, which Simon Baron-Cohen helps to break down in *The Essential Difference*. The systemizing male brain ("type S") focuses more on social class and hierarchy, and explains why guys so easily bail on their standards in the face of peer pressure. The highly empathetic "type E" female brain explains why women suffer more than men do when their relationships break down:

Empathizing is about spontaneously and naturally tuning into the other person's thoughts and feelings.... The person with the type E brain continually cares how the other might be feeling.... Women are more sensitive to facial expressions. They are better at decoding non-verbal communication, picking up subtle nuances in tone of voice or facial expression, and using them to judge a person's character.... Another difference is the concern that girls show about the current status of their friendships, and about what would happen if their friendship broke up. And breaking up is more often used as the ultimate threat: "If you don't do this, you won't be my friend." Girls, on average, are more concerned about the potential loss of an intimate friendship.... The female agenda is more *centered on another* person's emotional state (establishing a mutually satisfying and intimate friendship). (italics in the original)[5]

Girls are more concerned than guys about the loss of intimate friendships. Is it any wonder that girls experience a greater increase in depression when it comes to the ups and downs of their romantic relationships? The female agenda is more centered on the other person's emotional state. Doesn't that explain why women give in so easily to their boyfriend's pouting as he struggles to get past her sexual boundaries?

But there's even more to it. Neuroscientists have discovered that specific brain cells and chemicals are involved in attachment. After her breakup, Olivia asked, "Why do they tell you how to protect your body—from herpes and pregnancy— but they don't tell you what it does to your *heart*?" Another part of Olivia's answer may be found in a naturally produced chemical in the female brain called oxytocin. This hormone sends messages from a woman's brain for many functions—to the uterus to induce labor, to the breasts to begin milk production, and other things. But catch this observation from Dr. Grossman:

> More relevant to my patients at this stage in their lives is that oxytocin is released during sexual activity. Could it be that the same chemical that flows through a women's veins as she nurses her infant, promoting a powerful and selfless devotion, is found in college women "hooking up" with men whose *last* intention is to bond?...
>
> The release of oxytocin can be "classically conditioned"—after a while, all it takes for it to be released is catching sight of the man. Is Olivia avoiding class because seeing him will bring a surge of this hormone, a rush of agonizing feelings of attachment? (italics in the original)[6]

When it comes to treating women with respect and care, this is a critical difference between men and women that every guy needs to understand. Women are not like you. They are chemically designed to bond. And when you push past their sexual boundaries, you are causing them to experience powerful feelings of attachment and trust that are outside of their control. This is why the entire concept of casual or "safe" sex rings incredibly hollow.

Premarital sex is not just wrong—it's mean. You may believe the lie of safe sex, but believing it doesn't make it so. Your culture has sold you a bill of goods, my friend. As Dr. Grossman said, "Like it or not, hard science suggests that sexual intimacy initiates a trusting bond. Ask Olivia, who was woefully unprotected: there is no condom for the heart."

Where does that leave us as men? God created these differences and knew about them when He wrote the Bible, yet He never took the time to explain it to us. He simply asked us to treat our sisters like fine china and avoid premarital petting and intercourse. He figured that since He's our Dad and we love Him, we'd obey. That love should have been a good enough reason for us to obey Him, but for many of us, it hasn't been.

But now we've got an advantage. Now we've got the scientific evidence behind His commands. Will that be enough for us to finally change our ways?

Will it make any difference to you?

But she wanted it as badly as I did, Fred. You should have been there.

I've been there, and I don't deny that's sometimes true. But all that this "girls gone wild" argument proves is that girls are accepting the spirit of Baal right along with you and picking up the same kinds of strongholds of thinking that you are. Those shows and movies and songs and images that try to convince you that girls should be the sexual aggressors and call the shots in the sexual relationship are completely and totally false, and that *Sex and the City* idea about women using guys to explore their sexual fantasies with no more emotional attachment than a CPA filling out tax forms is downright ludicrous.

As guys, we often want to believe those lies, and I suppose that's why we like the visual paradise of the media in the first place, because it allows us to escape into a sensual, mental fantasy where we never have to deal with the consequences of our actions or the unfortunate realities that always encroach on our fun. That's where strongholds come from, of course, and that's why we're so sympathetic to the idea that sexually aggressive women are normal and happy and that premarital sex won't hurt them any more than it hurts us.

The trouble is, we don't live on TV and the "unfortunate reality" is that women were created to bond tightly to men. She doesn't come alive through the exploration of her sexual fantasies, but through a nurturing, empathetic relationship with a caring, protective hero who is committed to her and her alone. So when you run across a girl who wants it as badly as you do, don't think for a moment that you've enriched and fulfilled her when you've given her what she thinks she wants. That's certainly how it plays out on the silver screen, but our lives are real, and real life tells us the truth—behind every promiscuous, aggressive female is not a frisky, happy heart, but a wound the size of Manhattan.

That wound usually comes from her father. Go ahead. Test the theory.

Harsh, disengaged, and deplorable fathers are a rampant curse around the world, and many of us have felt those demeaning wounds personally. When fathers aren't who they should be for us, we all suffer.

My daughter Laura recently joined a holiday party with the young adults group at her church when someone suggested playing the game Would You Rather? Each player chooses a card with a question on it beginning with the phrase "Would you rather..." and ends with two scenarios to choose from.

"Would you rather live without music or live without TV?"

"Would you rather kiss a frog or eat a bug?"

They were all laughing and having a good time until the next card popped up:

"Would you rather live in a one-room house with your family for the rest of your life or never see your family again?"

"I was the only person in a group of thirteen people who said that I would rather live in a one-room house with my family for the rest of my life," Laura explained. "Every other person said they would rather never see their family again.

"People began to get uneasy. 'Well, I could still talk to them, you know.' Others laughed it off. 'Wow, wouldn't it be horrible to be stuck in a one-room house with your family forever?' That was definitely the general vibe going around. I was horrified. I couldn't imagine never seeing you guys again!"

Now granted, that's no scientific survey. But that's a pretty sad indictment of how Christian young people feel about their families. Could their fathers have something to do with that popular opinion? Maybe there's a clue here into what's behind the seemingly increased desire for sex—among guys *and* girls.

How many people would choose not to see their family again because of wounds or the cool disengagement they've endured at the hands of those who are supposed to love them completely? Every guy needs his father to accept him as a man and say, "Come up here and stand next to me in the world of men, Son. You belong here!" If you don't get that blessing from him, there's a good chance you'll search for your masculinity through the world of willing women and porn.

And every girl looks to her father to know if she is lovely. If she doesn't hear it from him, she's wounded at the center of her heart, and her response will be much like that of the wounded male. She'll turn to guys to hear what she missed growing up, as Jennie did:

My dad worked two jobs, and we had a large farm to maintain. My mom had a nervous breakdown when I was in second grade. She took a lot of medicine and slept away most of my childhood. They took care of my basic physical needs, but none of my emotional or spiritual needs. Nobody talked to me at all. I just worked on the farm, watched TV, and went to school. Neither of my parents told me they loved me until I was in my twenties, and that's also when I learned of my mom's breakdown.

All of my life, I just thought they didn't want me. I thought I wasn't worth being loved. It's been an eye-opener that Jesus could actually love me. As a young person, I felt like I would be just one of the quiet people almost hiding in the back corner of heaven. God actually wants to have a relationship with me? What a concept.

Somewhere between eighth and ninth grade, I lost fifty pounds and became 5'8" and 125 lbs. With a little makeup, I could easily pass for eighteen. I never had a boy show any interest in me before then, but boy, did everything start changing fast. I loved the attention. Unfortunately, all I attracted were the boys with low-to-no moral compass. Married men were even hitting on me. None of them liked me—they were just interested in my body. I felt like a naive lamb led to the slaughter. I once dated a guy who seemed honest and good, but looking back I realized he was heavily addicted to pornography. I had just decided that all men were like this and this was the normal way of living. Finally, at age twenty-four, I swore off all men.

But she wanted it as badly as I did, Fred. You should have been there.

No, she didn't. Her emotional wounds wanted it, to be medicated by the only thing she associates with comfort, that "love substitute."

What *she* wanted was a hero. She wanted a guy who would connect with her, not just hook up with her, one who would finally tell her that she's lovely to the core of her soul. She didn't want to be taken advantage of and further wounded by some guy living out his movie fantasies.

The wounds should put a new spin on things for you. Even if a girl seems to truly want it as much as you do, should you give it to her? Is that loving? Hear what Katie said:

> I sensed that I cared more about sexual purity than my boyfriend did, and subsequently, I felt a responsibility to lift him up to my level of commitment. Unfortunately, I stumbled down to his level instead. It really didn't take much doing on his part. I wanted to be loved and accepted, so I let him pull me down. It was simply more fun to have sex than to fight off the desire for it, especially since he didn't care that much about purity anyway.
>
> I wish now, however, that I would have been more open about my boundaries, and I also wish I would have walked away when I knew he wasn't on the same plane as I was. I lost respect for him as a man of God and, far worse, I lost respect for myself as a woman of God. There was no honor in our sexual relationship, and we definitely didn't involve God in our "fun."

Technically speaking, Katie's boyfriend didn't violate her boundaries because he didn't know she had any, but he still violated *her,* because God's boundaries are always in place to protect her, whether she knows they're there or not. Those borders are there for a reason, and you mustn't breach them, even if she opens the gates herself.

Once again, God confronts your will, asking, *Will you personally and heroically shoulder the suffering that comes from reigning in your sex drive and owning your sexuality, or will you pile onto My daughter's wounds and spread more suffering to the girls around you?*

I'll say it straight: you have no right to wound your sisters, regardless of whether they're willing or not. You must be greater than this, greater in honor and greater in your likeness to Christ. You must help your sisters to stand as you stand heroically with Him.

I realize that you may not be the one who wounded your girlfriend in the first place, but you're certainly responsible for her wounds today, because you're the guy she's with now. You're the one who can convince her that she's worth far more than the sex.

One guy came up to me and said, "My girlfriend is a good Christian girl, but for the past couple of weeks she's been calling me when her parents aren't home and asking me to come to her house because she wants sex. When she comes over to my house, she sneaks off to my bedroom upstairs. When I go to find her, she's all over me. How do I tell her that we need to stop having sex without disappointing her or breaking her heart?"

Breaking her heart? That's the least of your issues, man. You're crushing her relationship with God, and you're leading her astray from the only Person who can fill that emptiness in her soul. You're the one who needs to take the initiative here and stop having sex with her—you're the one.

And what if her father wasn't absent but was far too present, perhaps sexually abusing her early in life? Such women feel horrible inside, and all they want is your promise of love…someone's love…anyone's love. Pushing or accepting sexual intimacy with these vulnerable girls only causes those continuous waves of pain and hopelessness to crash on their emotional shores even harder than before.

Are you beginning to understand what sexual purity is all about? It's not only about being a good little boy and staying clean by missing out. It's more about sexual heroism. You can have real impact in God's kingdom, my friend, right in your own backyard.

Don't you see? Instead of being just another guy in the long line of those who will further wound her, you could be the one who opens her eyes and sets her free. Are you a hero to the girls around you?

You need to catch this very big picture: sexual purity is not about what you're cutting out of your life or whether God's grace will cover it if you don't. It's about what you are becoming as a man.

Perhaps it's useful to think about it this way. If you're a football lineman in training and lifting weights every other night for nine long months in the off-season, it's not really about what you've forced yourself to miss out on while your friends are hitting the pizza parlor without you, is it?

Of course not. It's about being able to defend your quarterback's blind side. It's about being that double-barreled destroyer who can smash the double team and pile up the bodies at the line of scrimmage. It's about being that clutch, go-to blocker who creates daylight for the tailback on fourth and goal.

Every. Single. Time.

That's the way it is with sexual heroes. It's not about what you're missing on Friday night at the theater with your friends or in the backseat of your car with your girl. It's about being the warrior standing in the face of enemy temptation, empowering and inspiring pure girls to be all they were designed to be. It's about being the guy who fathers *want* their daughters to be with, even if they've failed them themselves, and even when their daughters are lying wounded before you, completely at your mercy. It's about *being* a Christian, and not just seeming like one. It's about *being* a real man who God can count on to come through in the clutch for Him, no matter what the sexual circumstances.

You know, Jasen wasn't the cool jock who got to score the winning touchdown in the biggest game of the year like I did, but he was so heroic that he never left a girl worse off for having known him. He was never "cool" enough to have four girlfriends at once like I did, but he was so heroic that he never "practiced" on a girl sexually a single time in his life.

There's no doubt being cool is great for the ego, but being heroic has a real impact. If you're a hero, you leave every girl better off for having known you, protecting the emotions of each and every one.

Will you deliver what a woman really needs and longs for in the depths of her soul?

It's time we take a closer look at those needs.

8

HER NEEDS

Stronghold Myth #3: There are two kinds of girls, the kind you date and the kind you marry. But if you can, marry an experienced girl. She'll know how to keep you warm at night.

This is the kind of thinking women *don't* need. And once you've heard the faithful, vulnerable cry of the passionate female heart, this stronghold will seem increasingly shallow, twisted, and repulsive to you, and you'll want to tear it down wherever you encounter it.

What *do* you find at the core of a woman's soul? Far more than a desire to keep you warm at night. If you ever expect to capture the heart of a woman, you must first find out what makes her tick. That's what we'll help you do in this chapter.

God calls out to the heart of every girl and guy: *Come and live out what I created you to be. You're very different from each other, but that's all part of the plan.* We turn once more to author John Eldredge:

Permit me to bypass the entire nature vs. nurture "is gender really built-in?" debate with one simple observation: Men and women are made in the image of God *as men* or *as women.* "So God created man in his own image, in the image of God he created him; male and female he created them"

(Gen. 1:27). Now, we know God doesn't have a body, so the uniqueness can't be physical. Gender simply must be at the level of the soul, in the deep and everlasting places within us. God doesn't make generic people; he makes something very distinct—a man or a woman. In other words, there is a masculine heart and a feminine heart, which in their own ways *reflect or portray to the world God's heart* (italics added).[1]

The masculine heart bears the fierce, wild, and heroic side of God's nature. "The LORD is a warrior; the LORD is his name" (Exodus 15:3). That's why a man needs a battle to fight and an adventure to live, a place for the warrior in him to come alive, and that's why he thrives on being a hero to the one he loves.

The feminine heart portrays a distinctly softer, more vulnerable and more intimate side of God's nature, the side of His heart that longs to hear our voices as He gazes into our eyes when we turn toward Him. It's that side that yearns to unveil His matchless beauty to those who'll passionately pursue Him. Just like her masculine brother, the woman, too, needs a place to come alive, a place where three essential longings of her heart can be fulfilled.

First of all, as John and Staci Eldredge talk about in their best-selling book *Captivating,* every woman has a beauty that she longs to unveil. The deep cry of a little girl's heart is: *Am I lovely? Do I captivate you?* It's the kind of heart that called my precious Laura out of bed at two in the morning when she was a tiny girl to prance and dance before the dim, moonlike glow of her nightlight, twirling happily in her flowing, silky nightgowns. It's the kind of heart that drew my Rebecca to cobble together two trunks full of spectacular dress-up clothing and accessories to mesmerize Prince Charming—otherwise known as Daddy—many years ago.

But the feminine heart never stops there. For her, it's never enough to be simply noticed, no matter how dazzling or alluring she might be. She also longs to be fought for, to be passionately pursued by her gallant knight in shining armor, a hero who lives and breathes only for her. A good friend and study partner of Laura's once leaned over and kissed her in the library, evidently so captivated by her that he couldn't help himself that night. She was offended to her very core, inwardly raging, *You didn't even pursue me! You've never fought for me! How can you think you're worthy of my kiss?*

In short, the woman's heart embodies all of the beauty and mystery and tender vulnerability of God that we see in Him in Scripture and in the quiet moments we spend alone with Him in worship. She longs to be known by her hero, and she longs to be chosen. She's thinking, *Are you enchanted by me? Will you chase after me? Will you fight for me, my love?*

And once pursued and once treasured, she doesn't just want to ride off into the sunset to live happily ever after, reveling blissfully in her hero's arms. She longs to be caught up into something greater than herself, in some quest they can share together. Sadly, too often, we guys have made the girls themselves the quest, like that running back at Laura's graduation who planned to spend college flushing out coeds like hunters target quail.

Jimmie made that same mistake: "I was pushing hard on Tracy to give in to me sexually, and whenever she'd say no, I'd get furious at her. I wanted so badly to experience what my friends were experiencing with their girlfriends. Then one day, out of the blue, she finally said yes, which was the stupidest thing she could have done.

"I was *so* happy making love to her, but after we were done, I felt rotten for making her do something that I knew she didn't really want to do. Peer pressure got to me, and I let that quest take over my relationship with Tracy. We've promised each other many times never to do it again, but we can't stop, and now we're falling further and further out of love."

When we get it wrong and make the girl—or her captivating body—our adventure to live for, the relationship immediately slides down the slope. Why? You've lost your way to her heart. She needs to find that place where these three essential longings of her heart can be fulfilled, that relationship where she can come alive and live out what God created her to be.

But when you go too far sexually, you've swept that all away. You're no longer pursuing her heart, and there is no longer a grand adventure for her to be swept up in with you. Worse yet, now that she's unveiled her physical beauty, she finds that you don't care a whit about those deeper wonders of her soul that she longs to unveil to you. What can possibly stop that slide in the relationship now?

Are all girls this way? Although it may not seem so at times, I think that's how women were created. Sure, those longings may be camouflaged by her wounds, and she may sell out her heart and toss her body your way. As a result, she may actually think it's the only way to get the love she wants, or perhaps her heart is simply buried beneath the lies and strongholds pouring from the Disney Channel and Nickelodeon as girls like Miley Cyrus train her to stalk the love she longs for with songs like "I've Got My Sights Set on You." If she's watched the Disney Channel long enough, by now she may believe that her outer beauty is the only beauty she has to unveil, and as for her views on dating, she may think that sharing lives means sharing bodies.

But no matter how much her thinking has been impacted by the media and the culture around her, her feminine heart is still beating in time to God's design, no matter how faintly. Her essential nature and her longings are hard-wired in place, so if you expect to please God and deal kindly and honorably with the girls in your life, you'll have to handle their hearts accordingly, no matter how things look on the surface.

If I had any doubts about how a female's essential nature and longings are hard-wired into her heart, they were dispelled on a second trip to the Glen Eyrie conference center in Colorado Springs to teach and connect with another group of fathers and their sons. This time around, I brought Rebecca and asked her to share with the guys what their sexual purity would mean to the heart and soul of the normal Christian girls their age. Two days before, I'd marked a few pages in *Wild at Heart* and casually handed her the book, saying, "If you're having any trouble coming up with a direction for your talk, you might want to read these few pages as a guide for your thinking."

Ten minutes later, she bopped into my office and dropped the book on my desk. "Thanks for the book, Dad, but I'd already come up with all these thoughts on my own."

Hmm. I guess she didn't need me to tell her what she's living for, right? Of course not! She already knows what she's living for, because it is written on her heart.

To the audience of fathers and sons that evening, here's what she had to say:

I want to share about what your purity means to the girl you're dating, but let me begin by telling you that a girl dreams about her future husband a lot. He's pretty much the main dream of every girl's life. She dreams about a courageous hero who will always treat her with respect and love her completely, someone who will protect her and treasure her all of her life.

When you are in a relationship with a girl and are pushing her sexual boundaries or looking at pornography, you are not giving her the respect and love she's been longing for every day of her life, and you are crushing the central longing of her heart. Even when you just look at a girl with a low-cut shirt at the mall, you're sending her the message that she isn't enough for you, that she isn't the most precious gift you could ever have, and that she's not your dream come true after all. It's a terrible blow that will crush her spirit quickly, destroying her love and respect for you.

On the other hand, if you're being faithful to your girlfriend and are careful to look only at her and to avoid looking at porn, her heart will treasure you like crazy. Because of my dad's books, I realize the struggle that men have with sexual temptation, and how brutal the battle can be. If my boyfriend fought that battle and won it, he'd easily have my heart for the rest of my life because I'd realize the warring sacrifices he'd gone through for me and for our Lord. He'd actually be that strong, brave knight contesting for my heart and for our purity together. I'd know from then on that I could count on him for everything, as it would reveal his devotion and respect not only for me but also for his Father in heaven.

Always remember, a girl desperately wants you to fight for her. She wants to be the most important thing in your life. She longs to be wanted, she wants to be pursued, and she wants to know that she's valuable enough for you to take that risk. This point is so important that I can't stress it enough. A girl does not want to be the pursuer in the relationship. God gave that job to you, and she is longing for you to move in bravely and win her heart.

Great words, and well said. But let's go even deeper with this. Because I know that girls are a complete mystery to guys, I asked Rose if she would open up her journal to us so that you can get an even clearer picture of what God's called you to be in your girlfriend's life.

Take a peek into the secret chambers of the feminine heart. See the dreams, the hope, the beauty:

Three years before Rose met Jasen:

My Husband,

This verse is our promise! "And in him you too are being built together to become a dwelling in which God lives by his Spirit" (Ephesians 2:22).

Right now, as I write and as you are doing whatever you are doing, God is building us to come together some day and be a dwelling place for Him! Earlier this week, I came across Exodus 25:8, which says, "Then have them make a sanctuary for me, and I will dwell among them." We are those sanctuaries right now, but we are there alone with God, which is beautiful. Our single years are vital for us and our relationships with our God.

But someday, we will become one and our sanctuaries will join and He will live in us together. What a glorious day that will be! I believe all of heaven will rejoice and our Father will be hovering over us, so pleased with His children, so pleased that we allowed Him to lead our relationship and, now, our marriage! What a beautiful promise!

I love you with all of my heart right now. I'm waiting anxiously to look into your eyes and just *know* you are the one. I wonder if I already know you. I'm right here, waiting for you.

Amazing. Years before they even met, Rose was not only dreaming of the person she would marry, she was anxiously waiting for him and talking to him in her heart.

Think back to their wedding, the amazing presence of God hovering over the sanctuary to honor their obedience to Him. How'd she know it would be that way? Because she knew the desires and longings that God had for her and that He had written into her heart, and because she knew she wouldn't back down on the Lord's dreams for His little girl until she stood looking passionately into her hero's eyes.

Two years before Rose met Jasen:

My Darling, my Love…

I love you! Mandee got married a week ago, and it made me think of you. She kept saying how in love with him she is, and how he is her best friend. It kind of took me off-guard because I had idolized marriage so much that I didn't realize it was about being best friends with someone. But we will be!

I love it that I don't know who you are as I write this. But the Lord does. Isn't that fun? Yes, rather frustrating most of the time, but fun tonight. I'll enjoy it while it lasts.

We will have so much fun together! I can't wait. I've always prayed for a crazy life, a crazy love story. You're a part of that! What will it look like?

I love Jesus so much, and I can't wait to love Him with you. Maybe we already do. Maybe not, but you *will* love Him.

You will be a man of the Word, a man truly after God's own heart. You will win His heart, and you will desire to serve Him, not have Him serve you. The Lord will entrust His heart to you. You will be known as His friend, a friend of God. And He will show you His face and share with you the deep places of His heart. It will keep you humble before Him.

I long to love you and serve you. I am preparing. Come quickly, my true love. Come quickly!

Your Rose

Can you sense the purity of her love, her passion, and her hope? I want you to sense Rose's urgent longing to be swept up into a great quest together with her hero in the Lord's kingdom and the spiritual preparation she was making to stand gloriously at his side.

Three months after Rose met Jasen, but two months before their first date:

Oh, Father!

I think I really like Jasen Stoeker. Like, a lot! He is so masculine and kind and funny and good looking, and he has a solid character. Wow! Just the thought of him literally takes my breath away. I really like him. I just got his e-mail today telling me about his men's retreat. He called it a "manly" weekend. My heart went crazy! That is so attractive! He really is a champion. I could easily be nuts over him, Jesus. Easily! He is amazing.

Jesus, I want someone just like him. Masculine. Kind. Funny. Tender hearted. Teachable. Excellent communicator. Stable. Family oriented. Faithful with the small things. Tall. Dark hair! Dark skin! Strong chest. Financially wise. Hungry for more of You!

Wow, Lord. As far as I know right now, he is just what I desire! Oooohhh! Could it finally be? Maybe? Time will tell. I love you, Lord, and all Your ways!

Love,

Rose

P.S. Okay, Lord, I have no idea if he likes me. In fact, I don't think he does at all. His e-mails are so kind and detailed, but there's not even a shade of anything more than friendship in them. I guess he'll just never get to know I like him so much if he never tells me he likes me first! Hee hee!

You are good, oh God! And Your love for me endures forever! Yay!

Rose was waiting breathlessly for Jasen's pursuit, though her heart was going crazy inside. After years of waiting and years of talking to him in her dreams, his regal bearing was finally gracing her stage, but even then, she remained faithful to God's ways, disciplining her pure heart to wait a little longer. *Am I captivating? Will you pursue me, Jasen, and will you fight for me?*

He had to be the pursuer, no matter how much she ached for his attention. So she refused to flirt and didn't give him a single sign of her romantic interest. Of course, in God's timing, Jasen did pursue—and win—her heart.

From Rose:

I remember talking often about my future husband with my girlfriends and family. Some thought that I was crazy, thinking that this perfect man was going to drop out of the sky for me. They'd say, "Nobody's perfect, Rose. You're just setting yourself up to have your hopes and dreams shattered, or worse, you'll never even get married at all because no guy is that perfect. You're passing up good opportunities for the sake of ridiculous ideals, and you'll soon end up disillusioned by the reality of life."

Others loved my stand, swooning with me, "Rose, he's going to be so awesome!" I know my standards helped some of my friends raise their standards, and their hearts longed for the same kind of romance as mine did. Of course, there were nights—I know every single girl has them—where I just ached with loneliness, crying, *Lord, just bring him here! How long will you keep me single?*

But I refused to quit dreaming, and I refused to give up my heart's cry. I knew he was out there. That doesn't mean I expected to recognize him on the spot when I saw him. Sure, I always wondered if it would be love at first sight, and in a sense, it was with Jasen.

Then again, it wasn't *love* at first sight, not really. I simply spotted his *heroic qualities* at first sight. I think it was because I had seen so much that was *unheroic* through the years of dating that I could so easily see how wonderful Jasen was.

I used to have a list of the things I had to have in the guy I was going to marry. It made for a good starting point in my mind, but over time, my list got shorter and shorter until the list had only one line: "Does he love God more than he loves me?" I knew if he had that, he would also love God more than he loved himself, and that was all I would need.

While it doesn't look like much of a list, it was great at flushing out a guy's character by the second date—at the latest. You see, a guy's "cool" will grab your eye quickly, and I have to admit, cool is fun. A cool guy always knows the right things to wear and how to do his hair and knows all the right things to say. You have a blast on your dates because he always knows the fun places to take you.

But when it comes right down to it, you look at him and say to yourself, *This is great, but you know what? The Lord is not his first love. I may not know all the cool places to go, but I know the Lord, and I love Him, and I want to talk about Him. I want us to be challenged by the Lord, together. I want to grow.*...

It's so easy when you can boil down your list to one important question: does he love God more than he loves me? With that as your filter, it doesn't matter how cool he is. With that as your filter, he can't mesmerize you or blind you completely. The little things always give his heart away, and you can't miss them.

Say you're out with him and his friends at Applebee's and you hear the shady, inappropriate jokes they're making, and you watch how he's interacting with people. You can tell he doesn't love God above everything. If there are little children around, does he get down on their level and talk with them, or does he think they're a nuisance and ignore them? When he's in a group, does he take a seat or lean against the wall, tossing out "Hey, wassup?" every so often, or does he mingle with people, demonstrating that he is more concerned with treating people with respect than he is with looking cool? Does he offer a hand to help out when there's work to be done? Does he talk respectfully about his mother when she's not around? Does he protect his little sisters? No matter how captivated you are by his cool, he can't hide the little things that reveal his character.

A guy who loves God more than he loves me won't be dating me to validate himself because he'll have his validation already in the Lord, and he will be drawing from Him and serving Him. He'll never go out with a girl just to be going out with somebody. He'll have a certain kind of woman in mind, someone who is chasing after God like he is. There aren't two kinds of girls in his mind, the kind you date and the kind you marry. There's only one kind out there for him, the kind worth pursuing.

He will be reading Christian books and will be interested in learning and maturing. He'll have a teachable heart, spending time in the Word and letting the Lord write those truths on his heart by spending time in prayer. His conversation will reflect all of this as well. He'll ask leading questions like, "Hey, what's God been teaching you?" He'll really care about the answer, too, and won't just use it as a "cool" Christian pickup line.

That's what heroic is to me. It's not the candlelight dinners or the awesome drive around the lake in a black sports car. It's more like, *Can I run after Jesus as hard as I want to with this guy, or am I going to have to back down? Can I be what God's asked me to be with this guy? When it comes to his spiritual leadership, can I follow his pace, or will his pace be too slow? Is he really, really what I want, and does he make my heart come alive? Do I want this guy to be my best friend for the rest of my life?*

These questions reflected the deepest longings of my heart, and I suppose that's what made Jasen so easy to spot. When Jasen was still "the mystery man" in my journal pages, I knew he would love God with everything in him and that I would be able to admire his relationship with the Lord. There aren't many guys like that out there, but that's exactly what he is, and I couldn't miss it. He's got a deep well within him, and one of the things I love most about him now is that he's a man of obedience. He's going to live life, and he's going to come out at the end being the man who does what he says he'll do. I was amazed when we got married because I was expecting to be disappointed as I found out more about him. After all, people say that you only find out the bad stuff *after* marriage, but the more I got to know him, the more I realized that he was far beyond what I ever could have dreamed.

Cool guys are okay and an awful lot of fun, but I knew I wanted the heroic. Not all of my desires were perfect, of course. For instance, as I dreamed about meeting my hero one day, I remember thinking, *Oooh, maybe he'll be in a Christian band!* Since I love being the center of attention—in a good way, of course—I naturally thought he'd like the spotlight as well.

It turns out that Jasen isn't wired that way. He's more of a behind-the-scenes kind of guy, but he's crucial to the kingdom of God and to everything he sets his hands to do. As women, our eyes may chase the cool things in life, but our hearts are dreaming for that knight in shining armor.

Sometimes it's hard for Christian girls to realize that while they're looking for a heroic guy, they're also expecting him to be downright cool too. The thing is, if he's heroic, he probably won't be what you think of now as cool. But once you meet him, you won't even care. Your definition of *cool* will change. I know mine did after I met Jasen and discovered he was everything I wanted.

Most people who know Jasen don't realize what he really is. They see him as a computer guy, but he's so much more. Jasen has eyes for only me. He has no sexual baggage to work through, and he has no other girl he longs for when we're having a hard time. There's really nowhere for him to run in his mind. Some of my good friends thought I would never marry anyone, but now that Jasen's here, everyone understands why I held out for a hero.

From Fred:

Do you see now why it's so critical to give you a glimpse of the feminine heart? It's because our culture gets your eyes so captivated by her outer beauty that you can't see into the sacred place of her heart and soul, sculpted beautifully in her by the loving hand of God. Because of that, it's sometimes hard to see the girls in your lives as your sisters in Christ, but it's absolutely imperative that you do. Your purity rides upon it.

You've now gazed deeply into the heart of a woman and experienced Rose's dreams and hopes and passions bubbling up from the innermost springs of her soul. Now you know that there is so much more riding upon your spiritual strength and sexual discipline with your girlfriend than you've realized. She longs to find in you a man to honor and serve, a man who can lead. She's yearning for a shining knight, a man of integrity and honor and conviction, a man of the Word and of prayer and of worship. She's been spiritually preparing for years to be ready for where God leads your lives as a couple.

Are you spiritually preparing for her?

You see, it isn't about doing what you should at all. It's about doing what your heroic heart was born to do. When it comes to staying pure with the girl you're dating, it's not really a law issue. It's a love issue, a love for your Father whose nature she shares and a love for your sister and that vulnerable heart that beats for you, deep down inside her.

You haven't a right to touch her, that's true, but there's a bigger picture behind the rule. Who would possibly have the gall to use his girlfriend for his own selfish sexual pleasure after hearing from the hearts of Rebecca and Rose? Don't you long to be worthy of handling such priceless gifts with heroic care?

Recently, I overheard a Christian guy lamenting his current relationship. "I know we don't have a future together and I should break up with her," he said, "but I'm going to keep it together awhile for the practice."

I know this is a common mind-set, even among Christians. But tell me: how does this sound in light of Rose's journal?

Pathetic and heartless, isn't it? Now, look again at the stronghold at the beginning of this chapter: *There are two kinds of girls, the kind you date and the kind you marry. But if you can, marry an experienced girl. She'll know how to keep you warm at night.*

Sound shallow and twisted now?

Come on, you know what you really want in a girl. Be worthy of it.

Don't be warped by the world's thinking around you. Tear down your strongholds and seek the mind of Christ. Ask God to give you an even deeper revelation of the feminine heart. Prepare and become worthy of the beauty she longs to unveil for you.

You've got what it takes. You're His son…and until you fall in love and marry, you're her brother. So protect her like one.

9

HER DESIRES

Stronghold Myth #4: Women want a cool guy with a tight six-pack and a drop-dead grin. They want a guy who knows where it's at and how to show her a good time.

From Rose:

I'm going to take this one on. Actually, that is *not* what a normal Christian girl wants. She wants a man who is courageous, a leader, a pursuer, and someone whose heart is totally devoted to obedience, a man who is willing to take risks for the Lord with no guarantee how it will all turn out. She's not looking for someone who has it all together or for someone who always knows the perfect things to say. She just wants someone who loves Jesus and who is living his life for Him.

I admit that these are rare qualities in men these days, but they're irresistible nonetheless—at least to girls like me. Those qualities make it worth picking you over the "cool" guys because you have a depth that those guys have never understood. Most of all, those qualities make you absolutely worthy of a pure, godly woman who's *nuts* about you!

That's what we want in a man.

So what do we want *from* a man?

Well, the deepest cry of every little girl's heart is, *Am I lovely?* She wants to be pursued, and she wants her hero to want her. But how will she ever know that he wants her if *she's* doing the pursuing?

Perhaps you're asking what a girl wants a pursuit to look like. That's a tough question. The pursuit of a woman is a bit like a tennis match, except that the guy's the only one who gets to serve. Serving the ball can be anything, like smiling at her from across the room, striking up a conversation with her, asking her out on a date—anything outside of the realm of an ordinary friendship with her.

If she's interested, she returns his serve, keeping the point alive. Some ground strokes are traded back and forth, the point gets played, and then he serves again. In fact, he serves every ball until his commitment to pursue an ongoing dating relationship is clear.

Some guys may find that frustrating, like if they found out they had to serve every time they played a set of tennis. From her side of the court, she may wish he would serve up more often and at a faster pace. He may wish she'd return his serves more crisply, or even take a turn at serving a game or two herself.

But she can't take a serve—or start a point—until his pursuit is established, as this sets the foundation for the future of the relationship. This "pursuit" thing is very important to a girl's heart, and while I can't give you the exact rules to follow, there are three things that a girl should see and feel if you're pursuing her properly.

1. She won't be confused about your intentions since you've made them clear from the get-go.

2. She should feel safe, cherished, respected, and pure. She has a beauty to unveil, and you must be worthy. Your courageous pursuit reflects upon your spiritual leadership as well.

3. She should know that you've been captivated by her heart and that you've made up your mind to win that heart. She'll see your desire to find out what makes her tick as you search out her heart through conversations and e-mails.

Let's take a practical look at each of these three points, one at a time, to give you an idea of what a woman needs to see in your pursuit.

1. She won't be confused about your intentions since you've made them clear.

A girl has to know what you're thinking when you ask her out. Which is it?

Hey, we're friends, and I just want to go out to dinner for fun. Or, *You possess the qualities that I want in the woman I hope to marry someday, so I'm starting a pursuit to get to know you.*

Let me assure you, it's in your best interest to make your intentions clear, because a girl tends to overanalyze everything to protect her heart. She's asking herself questions like:

- Is he a man of God?
- Am I going to be enough?
- What in the world does he mean by asking me out?

Let me share a story with you to demonstrate how *not* to pursue. When I was attending the University of Northern Iowa, money was tight for my friends and me at times, so we picked up this line that we'd use when we wanted to help someone out by paying for his or her meal after church. One of us would say, "Oh, well, I just want to bless you. You can't tell me no because then you'd be stealing my blessing from God, who wants to bless me for blessing you."

This way, no one ever got left out of the fun if they were short on cash. We all became comfortable with this line and understood exactly what it meant as a sign of friendship between us. Comfortable, that is, until Danny used it as a line to ask me out on a date. I'd been sensing he was attracted to me for a while when suddenly he asked, "Rose, can I take you out to dinner and bless you?"

In this context, I suddenly found myself between a rock and a hard place. If he would have simply asked me to go on a date with him, I would have said, "No, thanks, I'm not interested."

But he didn't. He asked, "Can I take you out to dinner and bless you?" I'd been completely trained by experience with my friends to think, *Oh, I can't say no to this because then I'd be stealing his blessing from him.* Suddenly, his request had become a spiritual thing, and I felt like I had to say yes. In that split second of time, it seemed uncharitable and even mean to respond, "No, I refuse to let you bless me!"

But, of course, Danny was the one taking advantage of the situation. He knew exactly what he was doing. I'd never felt more manipulated. I'd already been friends with Danny for quite a while, and yet he had me so confused that I still couldn't be completely sure that we weren't just going out as friends.

Once we entered the restaurant, though, his intentions were confirmed. It turned out to be a double date with a couple of his dearest friends, and while I was acquainted with the girl, this was clearly not a four-Christian-friends-going-out-for-a-bite-to-eat kind of evening. It was a full-on Saturday night, double-date scene from start to finish. I felt tremendously uncomfortable because he was beaming from ear to ear since he got me to say yes to a date with him.

I was becoming quite irritated with him because he had tricked me into this double date. Under normal circumstances, I think it's really cute when a guy is nervous about asking a girl out, yet he courageously steps up to the plate anyway. This guy came through the back door by figuring out a way that made it impossible for me to say no to his "let me bless you" line.

I thought I'd given him the message that I wasn't interested in dating him, but two weeks later Danny called and asked me if he could bless me again! This time I said, "What do you mean by that, Danny?"

"Well, what do you mean by what do I mean?" he responded, sticking tightly to his ruse. "Can I bless you?"

"I don't think so, if what we're doing is dating."

"I just want to take you out to bless you, Rose," he said, feigning innocence.

The cat-and-mouse game continued until I finally dragged it out of him thirty minutes later. "Yes, I'm asking you out on a date," he conceded. Finally, he was clear about his intentions. Finally, I could say no to someone who was purposely trying to confuse me about his intentions.

When I say that a young woman wants to know your intentions right from the beginning, she simply wants to know whether you're requesting to hang out as friends or to go out on a real date. If you aren't clear enough about your intentions, you're being cowardly and manipulative to avoid the risk of getting rejected.

Ugh. When you stop to consider that the girl you're after has been spending much of her life dreaming about a hero who will one day sweep her up into a great adventure, being cowardly and manipulative isn't the best route to her heart, so don't try anything less than heroic. Knock clearly and ask boldly. That's what I loved about Jasen. I'll never forget the first time he called for a date and firmly asked, "Would you like to go out on a date with me, Rose? I really like you."

Simple, clear, and easy to answer, and I didn't have to wonder for a moment what his intentions were. If you want to bless a girl, give her a gift card to the mall. If you want a date, ask for one.

2. She should feel safe and cherished. She has a beauty to unveil, and you must be worthy. Your courageous pursuit reflects upon your spiritual leadership as well.

I first noticed Dustin at junior high church camp when my close friend Carrie spent the whole week hanging around him and his friend Billy. I never told anyone that I thought Dustin was cute and funny because I wanted to let Carrie have his undivided attention.

Fast-forward nearly ten years later when I was reintroduced to Dustin by an acquaintance at church when he was home from college. Dustin was hanging around our church a lot that summer, and when I planned a trip to a prayer convention in Minneapolis with my friend Heather, somehow Dustin and another friend named Jim ended up going with us. We all piled into my tiny red Kia Rio and took off toward the Twin Cities, where we all spent a lot of time attending the conference on prayer and hanging out with some old friends.

Dustin flirted heavily with me the entire trip, but I stuck to my usual routine and didn't give him a clue that I was pleased with his attention. But I did like the attention. On the way back to Des Moines, Dustin was driving for me while I sat in the front passenger seat. Heather and Jim had dozed off in the backseat.

Dustin and I were having a fun conversation as the miles passed by when suddenly, out of nowhere, he reached over and touched my leg, like, way above my knee! I about had a heart attack, and I was very close to informing him that he shouldn't touch me there, but he withdrew his hand. I decided to wait to see whether he would do it again. Thankfully, he didn't try that stunt a second time, so I let it pass.

Not long after that, Dustin invited me to a potluck at our pastor's house, and I ended up sitting at a table with Dustin and his parents. All three were paying such special attention to me that I felt certain he would ask to see me again.

Instead, all he asked for was my e-mail address, mentioning that he was heading back to college soon. Still, I was so happy he wanted to stay in touch, and I hoped he would pursue me because I felt an attraction to him.

He wrote me a couple of times after he got back to college, and I responded, but then I never heard from him again! It took everything in me not to write him again after he didn't respond to my last e-mail, but I figured that someone else had caught his eye at school and that it was out-of-sight, out-of-mind for me.

Sure enough, Dustin showed up with a girlfriend at a youth convention that I attended in November. I can assure you that they were being ridiculous with their public displays of affection. I was crushed. I was sitting with my friend Heather the entire conference, and she confirmed my suspicions that he was looking my way quite often, maybe to rub it in that he had a different girlfriend.

Toward the end of the conference, he had the nerve to approach me and try to talk to me as if nothing in the world had happened! I simply said, "Hi, Dustin," and walked away. He tried to approach me a second time, but Heather stepped right in front of him and literally cut him off! I love Heather! I walked away while she blocked his path.

Let's fast-forward to the next summer when Dustin returned home from school and was hanging around the church again. One night, a bunch of the college students were heading out to Applebee's after church, and Dustin invited me to join them. After asking who else was going, I agreed to go along, mostly because I was looking for people my own age to hang out with.

I didn't ride with him in his car, didn't talk with him at the restaurant, and didn't even look at him during dinner. I wanted him to know that I was no longer interested.

I guess he was a little too confident for his own good, though, as he gave it one more shot a couple of weeks later when he left me a voice message along these lines: "Hi, Rose, this is Dustin. I was wondering what you were doing tonight and wondered if you wanted to go to a movie or something. Call me if you have time. I might not answer, but just leave a message."

It was so half-hearted and half-interested, kind of like, *Well, I have nothing better to do tonight, so I guess you will do, Rose. By the way, you should feel honored that I want to spend time with you.*

Needless to say, I didn't take the bait. In fact, I was absolutely appalled! Guys, you have to remember that the cry of a girls heart is, *Am I lovely? Am I captivating?*

She can't take a half-hearted answer to those questions of the heart. Your pursuit may be a game to you and just another way to fill your evening hours, but it's all for keeps to her. Dustin only talked to me when it was convenient for him or when no one else was around. I felt so disrespected and unlovely, but I was grateful to know *one* thing for sure. He was not heroic, and he was not worthy of a relationship with me.

So I took my time in getting back to him. He didn't deserve a phone call, so I sent him an e-mail along the lines of, "I received your phone message the other day asking me to go to a movie, and I just wanted to let you know that I'm not interested in that." It was very brief and to the point, and I never heard from him again.

Again, Dustin's antics demonstrate how you are *not* to pursue a girl. Had he been pursuing me properly, I would have felt safe, cherished, respected, and pure. But I didn't.

First, I did not feel safe or pure at that moment he touched my thigh. Remember, your girl will have a beauty to unveil, and she'll be checking out your spiritual leadership. Displaying that kind of forward behavior injects doubt into her mind about the worthiness of your character., especially if it comes even before you've revealed your intentions.

Second, Dustin left my heart hanging more than once, and that was extremely disrespectful to me. I felt I was just one more fish on his stringer, and I didn't feel the least bit cherished. Remember, a courageous, proper pursuit is a reflection of your spiritual leadership and should leave your girlfriend feeling safe and respected always. If you begin pursuing another girl, be a man and tell her about it. Don't keep her as a spare in case that new girl at school goes flat on you.

3. She should know that you've been captivated by her heart and you've chosen to win her. She'll see this through your communication with her.

Your girl wants you to go out of your way to show her that she's the only one for you out of thousands out there. She wants to know that you've made up your mind to pursue her captivating heart and that you're definitely going to go out of your way to come around and be with her.

A real man won't need signals from her that she's attracted to him before he's willing to risk opening his pursuit. Only after she's sure there's a pursuit can she open her heart completely to you.

From Fred:

Let me interject for a moment here to say that it's a good thing Jasen was a real man because Rose was a master at hiding her signals. Like a seasoned third-base coach going through his signs, she held everything back. If you wonder what's going through a girl's mind when she's holding back like that, waiting for you to take the lead in pursuing her, pay attention to how Rose handled herself in the beginning of their relationship.

When Jasen became interested in Rose, he was like most guys. He didn't want to blow his cover unless he knew she was interested. But when Jasen put some tentative feelers out there, nothing happened. As far as Rose was concerned, he would get nothing to help him out.

Was Rose uninterested? Not at all. Actually, she admits she was quite en-amored with Jasen, and though she didn't yet know him well, she sure wanted to. She just had some firm views about what is right and wrong in dating relationships, and she knew it was best for the guy to be the open pursuer. He was, after all, supposed to be the spiritual leader of the relationship. She also knew that a good pursuit was healthy for the male heart.

Sure, she knew Jasen wanted to feel good and secure as he approached this uncertain new relationship. But because of her higher motives, she couldn't afford to worry about that. She was after *his* greatest good, as well as her own, so she played by a unique set of rules. She played hard-to-get for a while.

Rose wanted to make sure Jasen's interest in her grew from the passions of *his* heart, and not hers. She wanted to know—and wanted Jasen to know—that he was pursuing her for the right reasons, not because she was rolling out the red carpet and making it easy for him.

In retrospect, it brings to mind a game of chicken. How long could she—should she—hold out before she finally swerved? No one knew. But I'll tell you, I've never seen a girl throw out so much smoke in all my life. She even had me fooled, which is saying something, because I thought I'd pretty much seen it all.

Jasen approached her a number of times to chat and thought up innocuous reasons to e-mail her. He called her cell phone regularly to see how she was doing, and he even joined her singles group in spite of the half-hour drive from Iowa State University every Thursday night. Rose was outgoing and friendly, just as she was to all her friends in the group. But as for sending out vibes that she hoped Jasen might become something more than that…forget about it.

So Jasen backed off and shifted his gears into neutral for a while. Since she was showing no signs of interest in him, he figured she wasn't into him. He kept up the impromptu chats and e-mails, but he didn't continue with his plans to ask her out on a date until he could come up with a Plan B.

In the meantime, Rose was dying inside. In fact, one day I stopped by our church where she worked as the receptionist and chatted with her awhile. Jasen and I found out later that after I left, Rose ran to our pastor and pointed at me through the window as I walked to my car. "I'm in love with that man's son," she said, bursting into tears. "And I can't let him know it!"

We never heard about this until long after Jasen and Rose began dating because at the time, Rose was absolutely certain that silence and passivity were her best means of making sure Jasen was the one. How she held out under such intense emotional pressure, I'll never know. Finally, after about three more weeks, Jasen threw caution to the wind and tossed his cards on the table. He asked her out. He figured it was better to get slapped down now and get on with life than to forever sit at the side of the road stuck in neutral. Once he announced his intentions to woo her heart, starting with an invitation to go out for dinner, she simply smiled, as if to say, *Game on.*

Within seven months, they were standing at the altar pledging their love to each other "until death do we part." And Brenda and I gained one amazing daughter-in-law.

So what do you think about Rose's idea? It worked. At the time, I'd have bet the farm that Rose didn't care a bit about Jasen. And yet she was passionately interested in him. But because of her sacrificial motivations, she could not express it until Jasen decided to pursue. Remaining silent carried some risk because poor Jasen was left alone to wrestle with confusion for a while. But in her mind, that risk was the whole point. Finding out what he'd decide out there in the silence was the only way to ensure he would enter the relationship with a heart completely dedicated to winning her.

If you're thinking Rose is quite different from all the other girls out there, think again. As Jeff Feldhahn and Eric Rice's research points out in their book *For Young Men Only*, girls deeply want you to prove your true manhood. Your bold pursuit is part of that proof, and make no mistake about it.

From Rose:

When Jasen finally did announce his intentions, he was so heroic. He didn't just ask me out on a date. He listed off all these special things about me, and my heart nearly fluttered to a stop. I couldn't believe what I was hearing.

He told me why I was different from all of the other girls. "Your Christian character is great, and you are easily the most godly girl I've ever seen. If you want to know the truth, Rose, I didn't even know what I was looking for in a wife until I met you."

There it was, exactly what I'd been waiting for in my silence.

But at the same time, I got a lot more than I bargained for! Hearing those words almost scared me to death. We're talking really heavy stuff. But you know, I liked what he said. A lot. So there was no way I would say no to going out with him.

Now, that doesn't mean you're guaranteed to get a yes from a girl if you follow in Jasen's footsteps. But I'll tell you one thing: she will definitely respect you as a real man. If I'd have said no to Jasen because I wasn't interested in him in that way, I would have still ended up thinking more of him as a friend and as a man, unlike the guy who could only manage to ask me out so he could "bless" me. Jasen, on the other hand, stuck his neck out completely for me. He risked it all.

You see, it is only when you declare that kind of pursuit that we can open our hearts. I don't think you can be too early or too bold in declaring those intentions, but Jasen just about changed my mind on that score after we finished dinner and took a walk around Gray's Lake on our first date. "Rose," he said, "I asked my friends at Iowa State if it would be okay to ask you this next question on our first date. They all told me no and said that I would scare you away if I did."

My heart began racing. *What in the world?*

He continued, "But as we were walking, I realized that I have to ask this question anyway because I think it would be good to clear things up right away so that neither of us has any confusion about our relationship."

He paused for what seemed like an hour, and my heart was pounding like a jackhammer.

"Rose, do you just want to agree that we are dating until we either break up or get married?"

My jaw fell to the sidewalk. It took me many moments to process his question before I finally realized that I still needed to be polite and answer the poor boy. On the outside, I smiled demurely. "Okay, that's fine with me."

But inside I was screaming, *WHAT?!?!?! Those two extremes are so massively intense! And both terrify me to death!* I didn't want to break up with the greatest guy I'd ever been out with. But marriage? After having been on a date for only two measly hours?

But again, I loved it. I needed to know he'd been captivated by my heart and that he'd made up his mind to win my heart completely. Your girl will need to know that too, and if you need a little more insight as to why that's so, consider this final story.

Jasen and I e-mailed a *lot* as friends before we started dating, and though I gave him no signals, I was already swooning over him. Because I knew myself well, I knew I needed to guard my heart from this strapping young man in a whole new way. I knew how much I liked him already and how badly it would hurt if he went after a different girl, so whenever Jasen would write me an e-mail, I would read it twice when I got it (which was usually around midnight), and then I would read it once more the next morning. At that point, I'd force myself to delete it. I couldn't afford to read his e-mails over and over, or I'd never be able to keep my heart in check.

Once we began dating, Jasen mentioned an e-mail that he had sent me about his dying grandma, and I cried when I told him I had deleted it. (My computer permanently deletes my e-mails after a week.) I explained that I liked him so much and that he was sharing things that were so close to his heart that I knew I would get too emotionally attached to him if I kept his e-mails and reread them all the time, so I forced myself to delete them all. He was amazed, and he admired my self-control.

I told him I would give anything to have those e-mails back to read again now that we were together. Then he told me the most delightful thing! He had saved them all, and he would send them all back to me so that I could enjoy reading them again, this time knowing he was my boyfriend.

That was quite a happy ending for me, but the important thing *you* need to know about this story is this: you've seen that girls are more fragile when it comes to the breakup of relationships, and you've seen the reasons why. I wanted to share this story, to paint a picture of what that fragile heart looks like in real life, so that you can understand why it's so important to make up your mind and to declare your intentions clearly. She'll be trying desperately to guard her heart until you open yours to her completely.

Be courageous. Pursue her heart openly and guard it well. She's not just looking for a cool guy who knows where it's at. She's looking for a man. Be one.

DECIDING

Stronghold Myth #5: I need to date a lot now so I know what I want in a girl and how to win my bride when I meet her.

From Fred:

Having just been saved in California one year after college, I moved back to Ankeny, Iowa, and began attending church regularly for the first time in years. When I made my debut by walking through those heavy, ornate doors that first morning, I was informed that I'd entered the Sunday school hour. A kind gentleman showed me a list of adult classes that were available for me to attend.

I had no idea what I was doing, but as my finger ran down the list of classes, my heart was gripped by a description of the marriage class led by Joel Budd, the associate pastor. I'd recently come to realize that practically everything I knew about women came from one-night stands and casual dating relationships, so out of all the countless things that God needed to change in me, I figured this area of my life had to be the most urgent. Skipping from relationship to relationship had only spun me deeper and deeper into sexual sin, and while I was grateful that my selfish lifestyle had finally brought me to my knees, I knew that even if I wanted to date, I couldn't recognize a quality girl if I met one anymore.

So I headed off to the dating sidelines for most of the next year to sit under Pastor Joel's teaching. Come to think of it, I might have been the only man in history to attend a married couples' class for an entire year without having even one date! Over the next nine months, I listened to what the Lord was teaching me about that glorious creation we call women. The class was completely and endlessly enthralling, and I could hardly believe how little I actually knew about women after all the time I'd spent with them over the years.

I suspected that had something to do with my upbringing. While I was raised in a household of women—one mom and two sisters—they were as culturally bent and twisted in their thinking about relationships as I was, and as far as I know, none of us understood that women are truly a crowning glory of God's creation and that the Lord designed them to complement men in infinitely wonderful ways. I had so much to learn and so much to unlearn.

Gratefully, it was happening. By this point in the class, the Lord had the desires of my heart bubbling over with curiosity, and just before the ten-month mark, I prayed this simple prayer: "Lord, I've been in this class almost a year and I've learned a lot about women, but I've never really known a Christian girl like this. Please show me a woman who embodies these godly characteristics so that I can see what it looks like in real life."

I wasn't asking for a date, a girlfriend, or a spouse. I just wanted to understand women better.

God jumped right on that request—and delivered far more than I ever expected. One week later, He didn't just introduce me to one. He *gave* me one, the desire of my heart, my future wife, Brenda.

You know, it's funny. As a young man, I didn't start out "waiting on dating" like Jasen did. In fact, I chased girls relentlessly, like some gerbil on his exercise wheel. But in spite of all those years of endless effort, I never really found the girl of my dreams until I dropped my incessant "dating practice" and just began trusting the Lord to deliver on His promises.

When it comes to God's promises, do you believe Him? Somehow, Jasen always did. My son hung out all over town with the guys and girls in his pack, but he never went on any one-on-one dates during high school. One evening during his senior year, I asked him about it. "So, Jasen," I said in a casual tone, "you haven't dated anyone yet, and here you are getting ready for college. That's kind of uncommon. Any particular reason?"

He looked me straight in the eye and said, "There just isn't anyone out there, Dad."

Hmm. When it came to girls, he had his standards, and he was in no rush. Clearly, he'd just said it all, but I was so blown away by the maturity of his answer that I didn't realize how profound it was. So I pressed in a bit more. "Well, some of your friends have had steady girlfriends and all that. Have any of your friends ever asked you why you don't date?"

"Some. Jan asked me about it just the other day. But I'm glad it doesn't come up that much. The whole topic is just annoying."

"How so?"

"Well, Dad, people are so strange about it. They are all so convinced that high school is some sort of training ground for dating. Remember Mr. Peterson?"

"Sure. Everyone's favorite teacher."

"He's one of my favorites too. But I'd often hear him talking to kids about why it's important to date in high school. I didn't want to talk to him about it, but one day he and a couple of the guys cornered me. I knew they were only concerned for me, but they piled on about my need to start dating before I headed off to college. They said it would be good practice for picking a wife.

"I stood there patiently listening, while chuckling to myself inside," Jasen continued. "I thought, *If all this practice is so helpful in learning how to pick wives, why are divorce rates so high in this country?* But I kept my mouth shut. When they kept going on and on, though, I finally got so annoyed I blurted out, 'But *I* don't want to be practiced on!'

"You should have been there, Dad!" he snickered. "Their blank faces were hilarious! They all just stared at me. I don't think they'd ever thought about it that way before, that when you're practicing on girls, they're practicing on you!"

Thinking back on it, my face probably went blank when he said it too. I'd never thought of it that way myself. I admired his wise thinking—he'd reasoned it out on his own that he didn't have to date for practice, much less for entertainment.

From Jasen:

You simply don't need to practice dating to know what you want in a girl, no matter what everyone out there says. Dating is far too serious to play around with like that because of its long-term impact on your life and upon the lives of the girls you're dating. The best way to find a girl is to align your standards with God's and then set those standards clearly in your mind so that you'll recognize her when God brings her around.

I don't want to overspiritualize this, of course. I *was* looking for a pure Christian girl, to be sure, but I was also looking for one that could make me laugh easily, because I'd seen how awesome that was in my parents' relationship. It's not all about "deep spiritual seriousness."

On the other hand, setting standards must be less about picking *your* standards and more about lining them up with *God's*. Too many Christian guys remain blindly sympathetic to our cultural lies, so they're setting shallow standards like "she must be hot, she must be able to play an instrument, she must be intelligent, she must have a career, and she must be able to make lots of money." You aren't to pick just any old standards that suit your selfish fancy, just so you can check this requirement off your list and say, *Okay, Jasen, I've got my standards! I'm good to go!*

God's standards must dominate the process. You've got to desire what God desires for all of His sons, or these standards simply won't help you much in your search. While it may sound kind of strange, a good alignment with God actually made it much easier for me to *avoid* dating because my idea of the perfect girl made it completely obvious there was no one out there who matched that. I saw plenty of nice girls in the school hallways, but when it came to godly purity, none of them were overtly living for God and none seemed committed to anything but looking good or excelling in sports—sure pathways to becoming cool and popular. That alignment kept me from wasting my time with useless practice on the dating field.

Now, Mr. Peterson told me that I needed to be dating in high school so I'd know how to date in college, "when it mattered." But as far as I was concerned, it always mattered.

I didn't want to use girls for dating practice because it would be selfish and mean to toss their emotions around for my own purposes. And besides, I knew the girls were practicing on the guys too. I figured that was a good formula for failure when it came to my sexual purity, and besides, I didn't want to get emotionally wounded myself. Who needs that?

Of course, I still *wanted* to date. I was certainly attracted to girls, and dating looked like a lot of fun. But that strong desire is exactly why it's so important to start thinking like a man early on—when you're a teenager—so you can honestly face the facts about dating.

And here are the facts: At sixteen, where do you go with a dating relationship? You're still a couple of years from high school graduation and at least another four years away from a college diploma. That's at least six years away from being able to support yourself and a wife, and unless you're planning on getting married right out of high school (not something I'd recommend) and taking the first job you can find, you're going to be waiting an awfully long time to move that relationship forward. That makes it more likely that the relationship will fall apart sometime during high school, and because of that, I didn't think there was much point to dating that early.

I'm not declaring early dating a sin, but I am certain you can save yourself a lot of time and trouble if you'll just wait a little longer. In spite of what everyone says, waiting to date won't doom your skills with women. I promise.

Maybe the worst part about dating in high school is that even though you'll want to move toward a deeper relationship and even though you'll want to consummate things with all the physical privileges, God says you can't until you're married. The resulting years of temptation often lead to things ending badly.

You might as well enjoy high school for what it is without all the interpersonal complications, because the truth is clear: even if you meet Miss Perfect and start a relationship, at some point that relationship has got to stop growing because you can't take it deeper physically. If you're committed to sexual purity, you'll have to somehow remain content with saying no to physical stuff even as you're getting closer and closer to her emotionally. Can you be satisfied to remain extremely close friends the entire time, essentially placing your relationship into suspended animation for a few years until you get older? That won't be easy to do.

I did stay pure with Rose for our seven months until marriage, and with our defenses in place we probably could have gone quite a bit longer than that. But holding a relationship in suspended animation for six years? No, thank you. That would have been a long, *long* time.

Just to reiterate, I'm not here to tell you whether or not you should date in high school or even the early college years. You'll find many fine books out there that discuss the pros and cons of dating, including Josh Harris's books *I Kissed Dating Goodbye* and *Boy Meets Girl* and Jeramy Clark's book *I Gave Dating a Chance*. Get them. Read them. Consider their arguments.

I *am* here, however, to share the mind-set that was necessary for me to remain sexually pure from puberty on through to marriage, and I believe that "dating practice" in middle school and high school isn't at all conducive to purity.

Had I met Rose in ninth or tenth grade, I'm pretty certain I would have been thinking, *I'll try to be friends with Rose and do things with her in groups so I can keep in contact with her. We'll still get to know each other well. But beyond that, all I can do is trust God to bring somebody else of character into my life later or trust Him to keep Rose around until I can pursue dating her a few years from now.*

I knew a ton of people who dated through high school only to have the relationship fizzle out near graduation. Come to think of it, I don't know a single couple from my high school that kept the relationship going all the way to the altar. Those are horrible odds, way worse than what you'd find in Las Vegas. Why spend high school trying to beat daunting odds like those? It's not like you don't have other important things to do in school as you prepare for your eventual career.

My sister Laura picked up on that after a few weeks studying *I Kissed Dating Goodbye* with my dad. After he shared some of his choppy experiences of dating in high school and college, Laura simply said, "You know, Dad? I've been thinking that dating needs to take a much smaller priority in my life. It could take me away from my dream of being a veterinarian, and I just can't have that. Hanging out with guys in groups could be okay, but romance needs to wait. I don't really see what it gains me, and I don't want to risk my emotions on that right now."

Laura's thinking was right on the mark. There was no one out there for her anyway, just as there wasn't anyone for me. There will be a special person one day, however, so while she's waiting for her hero to ride over the horizon to pursue her, she's pursuing God and the dreams He's placed in her heart.

SHELTERED GIRLS

Once you've decided to drop the practice mind-set and you're in a position to date someone well, who do you pursue?

It's not good enough to look for a girl with the "Christian" label anymore because that name no longer guarantees much about her character or her commitment to sexual purity. Instead, you need to look for a girl who's in this world but not *of* this world. Garrett, a freshman in college, learned the difference the hard way:

> I made a decision early on in my life to avoid pornography and premarital intercourse, and I've stuck with it. Still, I haven't always lived by God's standard of not even a "hint of sexual immorality" in my life, but I'm now on a quest to make it that way.
>
> The trouble is, I have a girlfriend. She's always let me touch her breasts, but after a while I was convicted by the Holy Spirit and came to believe that's wrong. When I told her I didn't think doing that was right in God's eyes, she told me I was being far too strict. She pouted and whined, and I eventually gave in and did it again.
>
> Since she *has a reputation* for being a nice person and a good Christian, I showed her the Bible verse I found in *Every Young Man's Battle* that says petting is wrong. In spite of seeing the biblical truth right there in black

and white, she insists there is nothing wrong with foreplay. It makes it so awkward as the leader of the relationship to have her pushing so hard for these things. Most of the time I stand up like a man and tell her it's wrong and refuse to do it, but then she always claims I'm "pushing" her away.

Garrett *needs* to push her away. Because of the increase of wickedness in the media and culture, the love of many Christians has grown cold. They're not dead to sin (Romans 6:1–14), and too many are nurturing the ways of this world instead, allowing the strongholds of worldly traditions to dominate their thinking.

So again, you have to be more careful in who you're choosing to date. Garrett's girlfriend had a reputation for being a Christian, but reputation means nothing to Jesus, and it should mean nothing to you as you search for one to pursue, especially if you're committed to sexual purity while dating. After all, many Christian girls have a reputation for being pure, but they are still pushing sex behind the scenes:

> I know your deeds; you *have a reputation of being alive, but you are dead.* Wake up! Strengthen what remains and is about to die, for I have not found your deeds complete in the sight of my God. Remember, therefore, what you have received and heard; obey it, and repent. (Revelation 3:1–3)

It won't be her reputation or her family or church or school that makes her worthy of pursuit. It'll be her deeds.

If she won't agree to your standards of sexual purity, her deeds reveal her heart. Obey God and flee from her (1 Corinthians 6:18). She's the kind that the mediocre men chase as they're grinning, *She's the kind you date, not the kind you marry.*

If you want to stay pure, there aren't two kinds of girls for you. You can only date the kind you could marry because as a hero in God's kingdom, you're too much of a man and too much of a defender of God's truth and character to do otherwise.

Now, I had my standards for what I was looking for in a girl, and it didn't take long to know that Rose met the criteria. She had very high character and quickly supported all my standards, even when it came to which movies to watch. I knew she loved Jesus more than herself, and I learned that she would always put our marriage ahead of herself. She also complemented my traits very well, we were able to pray together extremely well, and we had a whole lot of fun.

But you know what? You don't need a list in order to spot a quality girl to date, at least not up front. You just need to listen for a little phrase out there. You see, most guys avoid sheltered girls, but I was actually looking for the sheltered girl, especially when it came to her commitment to God and to sexual purity. Whenever I heard a friend at Campus Crusade label a girl that way, I took that as my cue to take a closer look at her. Hearing that someone was a sheltered girl was usually a good sign that she was choosing not to do the things that everyone else around her had rationalized as acceptable. She was making a different stand, and I always thought that was pretty cool.

Whenever a girl's standards raised my curiosity like that, I'd start hanging around her in groups to look for the other things on my list, and especially to find out if she was any fun. If she was, I'd be open to asking her on a date to see if her reputation as a Christian was really true.

On dates like these, it's important to lay out your own standards and beliefs early on. There's no point in wasting time. Tell her who you are early and often, and offer her a place in your great adventure from the start.

I told Rose what my standards were on movies and theaters during the first week of dating, and I asked her if she'd be willing to live by those if we were to continue dating and eventually get married. I had to know early because that was a deal breaker to me. If she'd said no, I'd have had to move on because of what those standards meant to me. But Rose readily agreed to tighten up her standards to match mine.

The best thing about that discussion was that once I had that tough issue out in the open and out of the way, there was no doubt she was really special and quite different. I knew she was "dating material." We were not only on the same page at the start, but I knew we'd be of the same mind at the end if our relationship developed toward marriage. There would be no confusion.

You'll gain a lot by dropping the dating-practice mind-set, but it's important to understand going in that you won't be dating nearly as often this way. For some reason, some guys believe that if they begin to approach women heroically like this, they will suddenly become chick magnets around church, but that's not the way this usually works out. Patrick had this to say:

> In *Every Young Man's Battle*, it says that girls just want a guy that they can deeply respect, but this has frustrated me. I'm only fifteen, but I'm having lots of girl problems because of the fact that the girls I know deeply respect me, but they don't take me seriously as a potential boyfriend. They say they don't "see me that way."
>
> The way I see it is that these girls don't really want a guy who's going to love and respect them for who they are. They want someone after their bodies because they love the attention that gives them. Maybe that's just true of the girls I know, but it annoys the heck out of me. I'm not trying to use girls, but I'm getting nothing in exchange for that approach in terms of romance.

Look, becoming a rebel in this countercultural battle against Baal will make you a hero with God instantly, but don't expect every girl you meet to find you heroic. That news really shouldn't shock you. For one thing, many Christian girls are struggling beneath the same, warped strongholds of thought that we are, and so they may not even be able to recognize your heroism as the answer to their heart's cry, at least not until they tear those strongholds down. Second, not all girls mature at the same pace. Rose tells me that she was positively boy crazy at fifteen, and while she's nuts about me now, I doubt she'd have found me very attractive back in my sophomore year of high school. In other words, some of the girls around you may need to grow up a little before they can see your value.

I'm sorry to break it to you, but being heroic is not the way to speed things up on the romantic front, my friend. It's likely to slow things down. But in the long run, that's good: patience is the prerequisite for finding out who to pursue.

When it comes to romance, the question for you as a heroic man is not whether you're becoming attractive to masses of women. The question is, *Am I after God's purposes as I'm pursuing His girls, or am I after my own?*

Matt answered that question this way: "I've decided that I've spent enough time trying to get girls to notice me. I need to drop all of that and just bask in the glory of God while building up the guys and girls around me!"

Matt has discovered it's a mistake for guys to try to make themselves attractive to *all* girls. You only need to be attractive to the pure ones, the so-called sheltered girls. Remember, she'll be just as fun and crazy about life as the other girls once you find her, just like Rose and my sisters Laura and Rebecca. But you must also remember that many of these girls may be waiting to date until they reach college, so if you're approaching women heroically as a seventeen-, eighteen-, or nineteen-year-old, it may still be awhile before you're able to connect deeply with one of them. In short, they're off the market for now, but that's okay, because real men are patient and have other priorities while in school too. You can fill your time in many other fun and fulfilling ways while you wait. I had tons of fun in high school and college without dating.

The lack of practice never tripped me up either. When I finally did meet Rose, I knew exactly what to do to woo her, even without all that practice. As corny as it may sound, during those first important dates, most of what I needed to know about making a girl feel special came from deep inside my soul, bubbling up out of my growing love for her. When I needed further advice, I had some godly friends to turn to, and they taught me everything else I needed to know on the run. So, as it turned out, I'd been right all along, and Mr. Peterson had been wrong. I never needed any practice to know how to win my future bride when I met her. And neither do you.

These days, a guy searching for the girl of his dreams often sorts through women in the same way a boy paws through clumps of grass on his search for a lucky four-leaf clover. It's not about numbers, and it's not about luck. God offers us a better way:

Trust in the LORD and do good.... Delight yourself in the LORD and he will give you the desires of your heart. Commit your way to the LORD;

trust in him and he will do this: He will make your righteousness shine like
the dawn, the justice of your cause like the noonday sun. Be still before the
LORD and wait patiently for him; do not fret when men succeed in their
ways, when they carry out their wicked schemes. (Psalm 37:3–7)

You don't have to endure heavy two-a-day practices out on the dating field
to figure out what you need in a girl, and you don't have to put a procession of
girls through the pain of your stumbling "tryouts" to prepare for that special
someone *else*. God promises to give you the desires of your heart if you just wait
patiently—and purely—before Him. You don't have to worry, even if all your
Christian buddies are running around like the rest of the world, supposedly
practicing their skills. Be still and wait with confidence.

In the meantime, you can still spend a lot of time with girls by hanging out
with them in groups of friends. We all had a lot of fun this way, and I learned a
lot about girls too, without trashing their emotions or trying to take advantage of
them in the process.

Most of all, use your single years to become the kind of man worthy of the
woman of your dreams. While you're waiting patiently for the Lord to deliver the
desires of your heart, learn to delight in Him. Seek His path for you. Develop your
gifts, and set yourself up for the career He's gifted you for. Above all, don't forget
that God won't give His choicest lambs to mediocre men—so don't practice
dating. Practice manhood instead. She'll be looking for that evidence soon, so
you'd better be ready when the time comes.

What else will she be looking for? We'll take a look at that in the next chapter.

SPARKS

Stronghold Myth #6: Good sex is key to developing good romance, and the more sex you have, the more you'll know whether she's marriage material.

From Fred:

Let me kill this one straight out—good sex doesn't develop romance; it's the other way around. There may be no stronger myth that is more pervasive, twisted, and deadly to relationships than this one.

Many guys believe you can't measure the amount of romance and chemistry you have with your girlfriend unless you have a jumping sex life together. How *else* would you measure the sparks between you?

First off, the true measure of romance and chemistry in your relationship is in how well it fulfills the essential longings of the female heart:

1. Am I lovely?
2. Will you fight for me?
3. Will you sweep me into a great adventure with God for us to share together?

Look closer at each of these questions and you'll find just how much weight a physical relationship carries in fostering deep romance and scintillating chemistry.

1. Am I Lovely?

If premarital sex is all it's cracked up to be in romantic relationships, then hooking up should easily fill a girl's heart and keep her feeling always lovely, always captivating. Brianna told us that she has her doubts on both scores these days:

> My boyfriend and I were both active in our church: I worked in the church office, we were both heavily involved in our college groups, and we served as youth leaders and worship leaders. Heavy guilt overwhelmed us every Sunday morning because every Saturday night overflowed with lust, but it never seemed to be a good enough reason for us to stop.
>
> As a woman, I have a deep longing to be desired and truly loved, and so every time things got heavy sexually between us, all I wanted to do was snuggle and be close to him and to hear him tell me he loved me. Trouble is, once he had what he wanted, he saw no need for closeness anymore.
>
> It's so strange. When we were living the pure life early in our relationship, he would do anything he could to make me feel lovely and special, but once we started getting physical, all that stopped.

Hmm. The chemistry didn't accelerate with their foray into premarital sex, did it? It seems that the more they connected physically, the less she knew him emotionally. She didn't feel lovely on those Saturday nights, even as he held her in his arms, and she didn't feel the least bit captivating at church on the morning after.

Is this an aberration? It's not in my experience, nor in the experience of countless readers I've talked to over the years. But let's look at the second longing and see how well our physical passion fares as a measure of genuine chemistry out there.

2. Will You Fight for Me?

If premarital sex were truly a rich, concentrated potion for electric chemistry in a romantic relationship, then it would also be an irresistibly potent weapon in the hands of God's warriors for binding their hearts with the lovely, godly women they pursue. Yet the potion was more of a poison for Jake:

> I hope to have a daughter someday, and I recently and vividly realized that I wouldn't want anyone treating my daughter the way I have been treating girls—mentally undressing them, lusting over them, and getting them to do things that they normally wouldn't do.
>
> I can very easily persuade a girl to go further than she wants, and gratefully, I've finally started feeling guilty about that. I've also realized that God isn't going to let me meet the girl He wants me to marry until I clean up my act, because He doesn't want me treating His daughter like that.
>
> I sure get some grief for thinking like that. A girl from my dorm saw *Every Young Man's Battle* lying on my floor today and starting laughing at me for reading it, but I was fuming inside. People just don't realize what premarital sex does to a person and their relationships. I'm no longer friends with *any* of the girls I've had sex with. Not one. In fact, I almost hate them. Sex outside of marriage is unbelievably destructive.

Without the unshakable commitment of a solid marriage, sex is like that heavy cloud that comes over a hot, sunbaked land, promising a downpour, but then eventually blows right on by without a single drop of that refreshing rain you'd hoped for. Sex promises chemistry, and you can practically feel the lightning crackling between you as your eyes meet and you snuggle together. Trouble is, it's an illusion. The genuine chemistry never happens, the rain never falls, and your dusty relational landscape remains as dry as bones.

3. Will You Sweep Me into a Great Adventure with God for Us to Share Together?

Caleb and Lori began a great adventure, but the dreams died when *Lori* became the adventure, as Caleb describes:

Last year, I started dating the woman of my dreams, and I was sure I would marry her. For the first two to three months of our relationship, we didn't do anything beyond kissing. I'm serious. Her dad could have felt completely comfortable sitting in on all of our interactions.

Well, I guess I should have proposed to her right then because we soon started testing the boundaries together. After a couple of times I began to feel terribly guilty, and I ran from spending time with the Lord. That only made things worse, of course. I mean, how can you beat sexual temptation while you're fleeing from God?

Over the course of the next five months, we got into the habit of sleeping in one another's bed on a regular basis. Slowly, a cloud began to grow over our relationship. Where once it felt so free and easy to hang out with her, now our relationship felt so heavy that I just had to break up with her, even though I desperately loved her and longed to marry her.

When it comes to romance, the physical side of a relationship carries far less weight than most of us ever realize. The only impact it has on your chemistry together is destructive. In spite of the floods of conventional wisdom rolling in from our swollen and polluted cultural rivers, premarital sex actually *hurts* the natural development of human romantic relationships.

But how can that be? Knowing a girl sexually is the deepest way you can know her!

Nope. It isn't true. Take a closer look. What do you actually learn about a girl through this physical experience you share in the shadows?

How her body looks and how she responds to touch. That's it.

People say the deeper you get to know a girl physically, the quicker you get to know her heart. It sounds good, but these physical forays don't teach you a thing about her heart. All you've *really* learned are things that are going to haunt you later in your mind as you're trying to stay pure for God.

And what does that knowledge gain you anyway? All girls respond to touch in about the same way, so all you've learned is the one thing about her that is no different from any other girl you'll ever meet. What good is that? How can that lead to a deeper connection together? Premarital sex teaches you absolutely nothing useful about what makes her unique. It reveals nothing of the genuine inner value of her soul and spirit. Instead, it blocks the one avenue you have to search out those unique and essential things about her—spending time talking together and experiencing life together.

People also *say* that premarital sex shortens your trip time to the altar, but the most surprising thing is that it actually makes it more likely you *won't* make it to the altar at all. Why? Because study after study shows that premarital sex short-circuits the natural development of relationships. I've personally experienced that time and time again.

Why is this the case? At the beginning of a relationship, you naturally focus on the wonder of the entire person, and this causes you to dig into her personality, dreams, and thoughts, delighting in who she is. But once you leapfrog your way into bed, the number one focus of your dates changes to finding a quiet place to repeat that intense experience before the night's over, wherever and whenever you can. This greatly detracts from the true intimacy of the relationship by stealing the time needed to build it, and the growth of good romance and chemistry is stunted.

That's why Abby's story doesn't surprise me in the least. "I'm eighteen now, and I'm trying to get over a four-year relationship with Keith," she said. "I really thought we would get married someday. We had known each other our whole lives, and I always had such a huge crush on him! When I turned fourteen, my dream came true when he asked me to be his girlfriend. We had a lot of fun together, and our relationship was wonderful until we made the worst decision of our lives—to have premarital sex. Dumb, dumb, dumb! Everything just went downhill from there. He crushed my heart two months ago when he broke up with me out of nowhere. I didn't know what to do or where to go. I just wanted to die."

If you've had a series of broken relationships, you've probably assumed it's because you just haven't found the right girl yet. Are you sure that's the reason? Or could it be that you've been injecting the poison of premarital sex into relationship after relationship, killing them off with your own bare, groping hands over and over again? It's very possible, my friend.

If you really want those sparks between you to last, and if you truly want to know your girlfriend deeply, avoid premarital sex at all costs. When sex becomes your goal, sharing your soul will always take a backseat. You'll think you're getting to know her better, but it'll all be just a devastating mirage. Without a doubt, the biggest danger of sex outside marriage is not the risk of an STD or a pregnancy, but the illusion of closeness and intimacy that comes with it.

Over the twelve years Brenda and I spent teaching seven-week premarriage classes at our church, I suppose we met with and counseled two hundred couples. Invariably, what surprised me most about these lovebirds was how consistently deluded they were about the chemistry and depth of connection they actually had in their relationships.

At the first class we'd spend a good deal of the night allowing the new group of couples to get comfortable with each other. Brenda and I would ask some open-ended questions to get them talking about themselves and their relationships. Practically every couple gushed, "I've never met anyone I've felt so close to, someone I can really talk to like never before, someone I feel like I've known forever."

Of course, we knew something too. Every couple had to fill out a relational questionnaire for the pastor who would marry them, and there were some tough questions that they had to truthfully answer. From their responses, we knew that practically every couple in our classes was involved in some sort of sexual activity—and usually two-thirds of the couples had already experienced intercourse together.

But an interesting shift would transpire over the next two weeks after we handed them a copy of Norm Wright's workbook *Before You Say "I Do."* Nearly every couple was appalled by what that workbook revealed about their relationships in just the first few chapters. Their sentiments ran along these lines: "As close as we are, I can't believe how little we've actually talked about the critical things we need to know about each other for marriage. We had no idea."

All their vaunted intimacy was a mirage. They found that their "chemistry" was based more on the deceptive euphoria of touching and the breathless anticipation of their stolen moments together than on a genuine connection of their hearts and minds. No wonder our divorce rates are so high in the first few years of marriage. You wake up one morning and it suddenly hits you: *I thought I knew this woman. How could I have been so wrong?*

Just before I was saved, I was entering the fourth year of a relationship with a girl. Sure, we were close—we were even talking marriage—but I was gnawed by a deep loneliness I couldn't shake. About that time I met a French graduate student who asked me over to lunch, and I was so desperate to shake that loneliness that we ended up in bed that afternoon—and on many other days—over the next few months. I then met a local girl from the Palo Alto area through work, and soon we, too, were looking for every chance we could to steal away for some alone time together.

You would think that my loneliness would have been long gone, but it wasn't. In fact, if knowing a girl physically makes it that much easier to get to know her personally, those days should have been the happiest, most exhilarating days of my life. But I'm here to tell you they weren't.

All that "connecting" I did with them left me feeling like I wasn't connected to anything—even to these women. I couldn't understand it. Wasn't sex the quickest way to get to know someone? All I knew was that I felt like a gerbil on a wheel, running faster and faster, but getting nowhere fast. In spite of all the sex, I was even lonelier, bone-crushingly so.

It was like trying to quench your thirst with salt water. Why wasn't it working? Because sex outside of marriage is a mirage. It delivered no connection. The romance and chemistry that seemed so real were nothing more than the sizzling anticipation of when we'd next be in each other's arms. What a cruel illusion.

It's haunting to think I can still describe to you every detail about their bodies. I could probably still drive you to where they used to live, since I spent so much time alone with them in their rooms. Had you asked me then, I would have sworn I knew those girls deeply.

But if you asked me today to share one thing that made their hearts leap for joy, one thing about their dreams for the future, I couldn't tell you. In fact, if you held a gun to my head this very moment, I couldn't even tell you their names.

From Jasen:

As the president of my dorm, I knew a lot of guys on the floor were having tons of sex with their girlfriends. Each one thought he knew his girl's heart through and through, yet in the end, he would break up with her after a year or a year and a half when he finally figured out who she was and realized he didn't really like her at all. Sex dominated their relationships, and that physical focus kept them from finding it out earlier.

I always found this sort of stuff amazing. These guys wasted all that time and energy giving themselves away to somebody who they didn't even know that they didn't like. It never made a whole lot of sense to me, but it certainly shows how powerful the illusion of chemistry can be.

From Rose:

Some of our friends—well, maybe I should call them acquaintances—hinted that we would be behind in the development of our relationship when we got married because we hadn't had sex beforehand. But today I actually feel that not doing it gave us a head start over most couples. I knew Jasen was the guy I wanted because we *hadn't* had sex. I wasn't just hoping he was the guy or guessing he was the guy. I knew exactly what I was getting, and we never once had to worry about whether we were deceived about the depth of our relationship. That's because we didn't allow sex—and its illusions—to have a place in our lives.

Besides, avoiding the physical side of the relationship made everything a lot easier. We could simply relax and communicate with each other on our dates without dealing with the frustrating edginess that comes with wondering whether or not we'd get those physical desires met that night and where we might find to do it. I loved the freedom I had to find out who he was, what made him tick, what his dreams were, and what he was aspiring to be.

Sure, I was excited whenever I thought about sharing sex with Jasen in the future, but I also wanted to know exactly what I was getting into before I married him, and I knew that this would take a lot of time talking together and sharing our lives. I didn't want to marry him simply because we'd become comfortable with each other in bed, and I wanted to know for certain that he was choosing me for who I am on the inside, not for what I did for him sexually.

From Jasen:

We've never once regretted standing up against premarital sex like we did, although there were times before I met Rose that I wondered whether my standards of purity would ruin my chances of finding great chemistry with a girl. After all, all I ever heard about from the guys was that no one ever waits anymore, and all I ever heard from couples around me was how much electric chemistry there was between them when they were dating.

I couldn't help wondering whether I would ever experience that kind of chemistry doing things my own pure way, but I needn't have worried. It was terribly exciting dating Rose, and it wasn't a prudish thing where we didn't have any fun. The chemistry was every bit as electric as what I had seen in the lives of my friends.

In fact, the physical attraction is stronger today *because* we couldn't do anything sexual before. I think the effect of premarital sex upon your relational chemistry is a little bit like buying a new car. It's awesome shopping for a hot, gleaming machine and being swept away by all the flashy bells and whistles all wrapped up in that glorious cloud of new-car smell, but once you've driven your new ride for a while and tried out every cool feature, it's like, *Well, okay, that was fun. Now what?* It loses a bit of its luster in your eyes.

I think the same kind of thing happens to relationships, especially when you spot a hot girl on the school's lot and you're soon experiencing everything *she* has to offer physically. She soon loses her luster because the new has worn thin and her "cool" has become all too familiar to you. After a few more months, you're bored because those new, sensual features of hers were all there ever was at the center of the relationship. *Now what?* There's nothing left to do but look around for the next hot model.

That wasn't an issue for us because our chemistry never revolved around our bodies. A good, strong interpersonal chemistry does develop without those physical things. Mystery, excitement, and delayed gratification are the very core of romance! Best of all, unlike the sexual chemistry that weakens with boredom, our chemistry seemed to grow the entire time we were dating and right on through the engagement to our wedding day. That strong, physical desire and the mystery surrounding sex always remained with us, and that spark kept flashing all the way to the altar.

Some might portray our path as boring, thinking our standards stole all the fun out of life. But we enjoyed our times together like crazy, every step of the way, and we absolutely love how things have turned out for us in marriage.

We're hoping you'll choose to stir up chemistry with your girlfriend like we did, without filling your days and nights with all those physical passions. If you follow our lead, then you'll need to fill your times with other things, so let me give you some advice. On our early dates, we sometimes found it difficult to think of something fun to do off the top of our heads, so I sat down with Rose and put together a list of dates that sounded interesting and enjoyable and would keep us out in public where sexual temptation would be far from our minds.

You'll need to sit down and create a list of your own, of course, but take a look at a portion of ours:

- Walk around campus
- Visit Amana Colonies
- Check out the Iowa State Fair
- Be extras in a movie together
- Fly a kite
- Go on a picnic
- Go to a state park
- Go on a road trip
- Go for burritos
- Go to the International House of Prayer
- Go roller skating
- Get pictures taken in a mall photo booth
- Dance Dance Revolution™
- Watch a favorite movie
- Play a board game

- Visit the old houses where we grew up
- Go on a double date with each set of parents
- Go on a double date with a pastor and his wife
- Play Truth or Dare in public (it's riskier that way!)
- Swing on a swing set
- Bake a cake
- Go on a long bike ride
- Go to an amusement park
- Visit Virtual Reality Applications Center at ISU
- Draw/paint portraits of each other
- Go cloud chasing
- Go to Barnes & Noble to browse
- Go ice skating
- Go to a musical, symphony, or show
- Go-karts!
- Have a picnic by the airport to watch planes
- Go to a school production or sporting event
- Walk in the rain, splash in puddles, drink hot cocoa
- Learn a new skill from each other
- Make a gourmet meal
- Have a photo day using up disposable cameras
- Follow a random person without getting caught
- Go disc-golfing
- Go to a library and pick books to read to each other
- Rent costumes and go to a restaurant
- Go canoeing
- Listen to "our song" in a new place
- Go to our wedding together (added the day I proposed!)

From Fred:

What really defines a dating relationship? What is the difference between a dating relationship and simple friendship?

Some believe it's the kissing and sex. From time to time, I get e-mails from guys who tell me that they've taken a fresh stand for purity in their relationships with their girlfriends, only to have the girls respond, "That's not good enough for me. I need more touching or it doesn't feel like we're in love." Our culture constructs these strongholds of thought quite easily these days. While it's a horrifying attitude to God, many Christians are sympathetic to the Enemy's lie that the physical side of your relationship must be given a good deal of weight when it comes to choosing your mate.

I don't agree that it's the kisses and sex that define the difference between a dating relationship and a good friendship with a girl. It's the romantic chemistry that defines the difference, a chemistry that grows from a commitment to knowing each other deeply. Can you have romantic chemistry without getting physical? Of course you can! As guys, we'd all do well to appreciate that more mysterious, deeper kind of chemistry that our girlfriends and wives seem to understand implicitly.

I can't help recalling what Rose wrote in her journal two years before she met Jasen: "I've always prayed for a crazy life, a crazy love story." Can you have a crazy love story and crazy romantic chemistry without sex? Rose has offered to share a few stories from her and Jasen's dating days. I'll let you be the judge:

Place: Palmer's Deli & Market, West Des Moines, Iowa
Date: The First Month of Dating

It was my first time at a Palmer's Deli, and I was blown away by the sensory overload. There were four separate lines for ordering soups, salads, sandwiches, and sides, and countless confusing menu boards hanging from every wall and rafter. Yet somehow, everyone managed to get their plates and bowls filled while funneling their way down to a single cash register. I couldn't for the life of me figure out how to order, so I was happy to let Jasen take the lead.

We were standing at the soup counter, and Jasen was ordering when I happened to glance up at him. I was swept away by his good looks! The sights and sounds around me completely disappeared as I swooned, thinking to myself, *I can't believe I am dating him! He is so handsome and so wonderful and kind and sweet and polite. I just can't believe I'm with him and none of these other girls are. He's so good looking.*

The next thing I knew, Jasen had turned to look at me with a grin. The sounds of the restaurant began to slowly get louder when I was suddenly snapped back to reality by the man behind the soup counter saying, "Ma'am? Ma'am? Excuse me, ma'am!"

I jerked my head around to look at him blankly. He burst out laughing, and so did Jasen. I'd been in a daze staring at Jasen—and I'd gotten caught! I was terribly embarrassed, and I tried to just brush it off casually, but Jasen would have none of that. He just couldn't pass up such a great opportunity to tease me, and, of course, he was feeling pretty special.

"Were you staring at me, Rose?" he said, winking.

And his grin stole my heart away again. I blushed more than I ever have in my entire life, and I gave him his self-esteem boost of the year! I told him I was lost in thought about how handsome he was and how I literally didn't hear anything in the restaurant for several moments. I could only hear my own thoughts and my heart fluttering. Needless to say, he still loves to hear me tell that story—again and again. And again.

Place: Downtown Des Moines, Iowa
Date: The First Month of Dating

We were walking through the skywalks in downtown Des Moines when I asked if we could skip down to the street level to look up at the forty-four-story Principal Building because I love to crane my neck to see how tall it is.

While we were down there, I suddenly remembered hearing from friends that it's really fun to lie down on the sidewalk and look up at the building. I excitedly told Jasen about my idea and how I'd always wanted to do it but had never done it before. Before I knew it, he grabbed my hand and dropped to his back on the sidewalk! My jaw fell open as I saw him do it, and suddenly I was being pulled down with him.

I was ecstatic! We lay there for a few minutes, laughing. There were a lot of people walking by, staring at us in disbelief. I loved his sense of adventure, but do you know what I loved the most? I knew he did it just for me!

Place: Rose's House, Ankeny, Iowa
Date: Two Months Before Our First Date

Soon after meeting Jasen, I noticed a pattern to his e-mails very quickly—he always seemed to write me around midnight. I had to get up early for work, so I would go to bed and fall asleep, but I kept my laptop right there in bed with me. Around midnight, I would either wake up automatically or, as it was on most nights, I'd still be awake at twelve just thinking about Jasen and anticipating his e-mail, watching the clock tick through to midnight.

The moment midnight arrived, I'd hurry and get online and check for an e-mail from him. Even now, I can still feel the soaring in my heart when I think about seeing his name in dark, bold print, signaling that unopened e-mail. Once we were engaged, I actually asked Jasen to send me one of his e-mails a second time, just so that I could leave it unopened in my inbox so that I could always see his name in that dark, bold print and feel that special feeling. To this day, I look forward to opening my in-box just so I can remember what it was like to get new e-mails from him early in our relationship.

An excerpt from an early e-mail to Jasen (I saved giving him this one until after we were married, figuring it was too much to reveal that early in the relationship):

> You are so amazing, Jasen. I am so thankful that God has allowed me to be
> dating you, and today it was brought home to me with an even deeper
> awareness. Today Tony came into the church to meet with Pastor Dave for
> counseling. Tony began pursuing me last fall, and I'm pretty sure he still
> likes me because he once told me that he actually liked me from the first
> time he saw me in the spring a little over a year ago, right after I moved

back from Kansas City. He finally got up the courage to begin pursuing me that fall.

I told him at the time that I was not interested in entertaining him as more than a friend, but my family and friends suggested that I at least give him a chance since he is a Christian and has a good job and a good reputation, all the things that help make for a good husband. I finally agreed to go out on a date with him in January, and we spent the weekend together, going out on Friday night, Saturday night, and then for lunch on Sunday. It was a lot like the kind of weekend you and I just spent together.

Jasen, I am now nearly in tears as I type this. He is sitting in the next room over from me right now. I couldn't feel more distant from him, and I couldn't want him to be any farther away than I want him to be right now. You are in Cedar Rapids, and I couldn't feel closer to you. I don't think I could want you closer to me than I want you to be right now.

When our wonderful weekend first started on Friday night, even before you got to my house (actually, since you called me on Tuesday and asked me out on a date), I couldn't get the butterflies to stop fluttering around my stomach! When we ate dinner at Lone Star on Friday night, I ate more that night than I had eaten all week since Tuesday night! I just couldn't eat because I was so excited and nervous and full of anticipation. I couldn't *wait* to see you. I spent three hours getting ready for you, and I nearly flipped out when I saw you pull into my driveway.

When Tony was coming to pick me up for our first date in January, I was dreading it. I almost wore a sweatshirt because I didn't have any desire to get dressed up for him. I was nervous, but it was a dreadful nervousness. When he picked me up, my heart didn't move at all.

We went out, and we talked, and it was fun because I'm good at making people feel at ease, but I had to do most of the work. He asked questions, and we had a good conversation, but I felt like I was there doing my duty, not feeling like a princess. We had already made plans to hang out with another couple after church the next night, and I didn't want to go!

I hated seeing him in church, I hated that he came and sat by me after the service, and then I hated it when he came and prayed for me at the altar.

I hated every second of it. When you prayed for me that night that I was crying in the sanctuary, I couldn't have felt safer. But when Tony laid his hand on my shoulder to pray for me, it didn't feel right at all, even though I knew that in his heart he adored me. He really did.

He's really a great guy, and he would have been a great catch for me in many people's eyes, but my heart just wasn't in it. I remember crying to God, asking Him why He wouldn't just let me fall in love with Tony, because he was about the fourth great Christian guy I had turned down. I was so frustrated with choosing to remain single, because I so deeply desired a husband. (By the way, he just left Pastor Dave's office and walked by my desk and smiled at me. I'll look at my picture of you instead!)

But my heart just wouldn't let me choose him, or any of the others. I remember feeling so hopeless and scared because all I ever wanted was to be adored and cherished, and here was a great man of God offering me exactly that. But whenever I looked at him throughout that weekend with him, I realized I had deep desire burning in my heart that I wasn't even aware of until then.

I desired to adore someone! I desired to be absolutely nuts about one of God's sons. I wanted to be absolutely crazy about the guy who was nuts about me. And every time I looked at him, I knew I wasn't crazy about Tony. I tried to make myself be crazy for him, but I couldn't betray my heart.

So I drove over to his house, and I told him that I couldn't date him and that I could never be more than his friend. He was devastated and so was I, but I remember feeling so free after I left to head home. Free, yet terrified at the same time, because I realized that I was asking God for such a huge, specific, practically impossible thing—to deliver a guy I was absolutely crazy over.

Before I even got home I just decided to stop looking for a guy, and

I decided to pursue missions instead. I figured that if God wanted to drop a man in my life, He could do it, but since that would take such a miracle, I was done trying to make something happen on my own. I figured it would take God at least three years to make something of this magnitude happen in my life.

Then I met you, Jasen. It didn't even take three months. I still have no idea where this whole thing is going, but I do know that my heart is going crazy again, and that I haven't ended up alone for the rest of my life after all. I didn't have to settle for one of the great guys around here. God handed me the best!

You are everything I have ever wanted. I don't know yet if you will be my husband, as that is for God to reveal sometime in the future, but I do know that if this is nothing but a friendship, I will forever look at you as a gift from God. You are a breath of fresh air from heaven, reassuring my heart that I will indeed love again, and be loved. I will know, and I will be known. Oh, how I pray it will be you! You are everything I want, Jasen. Yes, everything, right on down to your dark hair and strong, puffy chest!

I don't regret saying no to the others, and I don't regret the scary, lonely nights, wondering if I had just passed up the last guy who would ever adore me. I don't regret taking that risk, especially since I've met you.

Thank you for taking an interest in me, and thank you for asking our Father if He would entrust you with me. I still don't know if He'll answer yes or no, but I trust Him with my whole heart, and I trust Him with yours. I desire you to be *so* overwhelmed with His goodness, and if I am a part of that, it would be the greatest honor of my life, just short of the honor of belonging to the Lord Himself.

Anyway, I just wanted to let you know that I was thinking about you this day and I am amazed at who you are. You are a hero, Jasen. And I am absolutely honored to have known you!

His Beloved,

Rose

So Rose has shared her stories. What do you think? Can you have a crazy love story and crazy romantic chemistry without sex?

Apparently, romantic chemistry is *not* born of the intense, edgy, I-just-can't-keep-my-hands-off-you passion of the late-night hours, no matter what you've heard. Genuine chemistry is spawned as your own pure, irresistible, heroic character answers the deepest cry of her yearning heart. *Yes, you are lovely, and I'll fight to pursue you instead of my passions, so that I might know every intimate detail of the captivating inner beauty you have to unveil.*

Once again, the world's consensus is wrong, and a bow to Baal's idol offers you no more chemistry than flashy, empty promises. So what will you do? Sooner or later, God will challenge your will as you stand with your girl before that tree in the middle of the garden. *Will you choose Me and My promised blessing, or will you choose her body? Will you tear down this myth that stands between us and My dreams for My daughter? Or will you choose your own way?*

His promises are true, so choose well. As you do, be sure to invite her to join the adventure with you. That's what we'll talk about in the next chapter.

12

TRAIN HER WELL

Stronghold Myth #7: You can't afford to be too vocal or rigid about your standards and boundaries in your relationship. That just makes you look weak to her, and besides, she'll have her own set of opinions on all this. If she's ready and willing for something physical, you'll hurt her feelings and drive her away when you refuse. How can you influence her toward Christ after she's gone?

From Fred:

Who taught you this? God teaches us differently. If you want to influence her for the good, your first responsibility as a Christian witness is to obey Him: "Flee from sexual immorality" (1 Corinthians 6:18).

Obedience is always your best witness, and setting boundaries—or lines of demarcation—is your fastest way to flee from sexual immorality.

How badly do you want to stay pure? If you're heroic, you'll protect your relationship with all your heart, mind, and strength. And that means you'll set the boundaries early in the game. In fact, the earlier, the better.

You have to understand how the body works. Each sensual act is designed to sweep you deeper toward the next one as the body prepares for sexual intercourse.

There are only thin boundary lines between a peck, a kiss, heavy necking, and petting, and the move from one to the next happens exceedingly fast. Believe me and billions of other guys before you: a simple frontal hug or her hand laid innocently on your thigh can ignite the cascade.

It's both sad and embarrassing how many single Christian guys have told me, "Why couldn't I stop? I've already done everything with my girlfriend short of intercourse. What was wrong with my will?"

There was nothing wrong with their will, because premarital sex has little to do with your will once you're in the backseat of your car, cuddling up. Once your body grabs the reins, it's all over, because racing through the lines is simply the way your body is built to work. Deep down, your will joins the mutiny, intensely hoping that she'll give you the green light to push your passions over the edge.

Your will must come into play much earlier, when you can still set up your defenses ahead of time and cut your rebellious body off at the pass. You ignore these truths at your own peril.

Any useful defense must start with a frank discussion between you and your girlfriend about where the boundaries will lie in your relationship. If you don't know what she's thinking, you've set yourself up for failure. As a hero, knowing what she needs you to protect should be the strongest deterrent you have to your body's influences. Without setting firm boundaries, you'll be fumbling around in the heat of the moment trying to guess where the lines are, rationalizing all the way.

You must talk about these boundaries as early in the relationship as possible, but most guys never get around to doing this. Others wait too long out of fear of looking weak, looking like a sissy, or driving the girl away from the start. But remember, a real man gets his validation from God, not women. If the girl doesn't respond positively to your request to discuss boundaries, that's no reflection upon your manhood. She simply isn't the girl you want to be with. After all, you're a sexually pure hero of God pursuing a certain kind of girl, and God's with you in the pursuit. He's got another girl out there for you somewhere, so trust Him. It's time to man up and move on.

Do you remember the one item Rose had on her list of qualities that she had to have in the man she married? In case you've forgotten, here it is again: Does he love God more than he loves me?

That makes a pretty good pop quiz question for you, so here it is: do you love God more than you love the girl you're dating? If she's got a normal feminine heart, that's what she wants most in a guy, and nothing will make you more attractive than standing up courageously and laying out the standards you will live by. That's one way to show her that you love God more than you love her, but it's also a good way to filter out the girls who will threaten your purity before God. There's nothing more dangerous to your sexual purity than dating a girl who doesn't really care about it, and you'd better discover that danger at the start.

Like many guys, you may think that such a conversation will be awkward or awful. Judging from the conversation I had recently with a fellow named Josh, he'd been way off in his thinking like this too. Josh, a high school senior, told me that he'd been dating a Christian girl for seven months. "But we've been struggling with our purity," he said. "The primary reason is because I've been embarrassed to tell her that certain things we do cause lust problems in my mind. Some of them seem like such small things, like kisses that last too long. But do you know what I just did last week? I told her that for the next month I wanted us to go on a fast from making out and see where that might lead us spiritually. I also confessed that it had been too difficult for me to keep my mind from stumbling and that I was trying to raise the bar on my sexual purity."

"Awesome!" I said. "Way to go, Josh!"

"The whole thing has surprised me so much!" he beamed. "I can't express how free I feel and how much more manly I feel. My self-image has taken a huge leap overnight."

God is renewing Josh's mental image of manhood to one of a warrior who fights for his King, which shouldn't surprise you. You're a man, and it's your job to set the standards—and defend them. You'll always feel manly when you're doing a man's work. Your heart is built that way.

That doesn't mean that every girl will understand your passion for God's ways, of course. Again, even the minds of Christian girls have been twisted by

Baal's touch these days. Alec said he told his girlfriend recently that they would have to lay off the touching and feeling because the Lord was changing his thinking about sexual purity. "She got angry with me, and she wasn't very understanding at all," Alec said. "She says she can't be around me unless I go back to the way I was."

Alec wasn't expecting this reaction from his girlfriend at all. "She says she still wants to keep dating, but right now she can't handle being near me without touching me," he explained.

Alec's dilemma illustrates again why it's so important to have these boundary discussions early in a relationship. I know too many guys who are afraid their standards will be deal breakers, so they put off these discussions, thinking, *Well, if we can date long enough, she'll find enough good things that she likes about me that she'll put up with my standards. Better that way than having her dump me now.*

Be a man. Go ahead and let her tell you that the relationship won't work out or that she wants to move on. Sure, that'll sting, but you're a man with standards, and those standards are a protective shield for the both of you. You need a woman who'll keep pace with you, not one who'll simply put up with your standards against her will. I don't care how attractive she is, she's not the one for you. Trust God to bring another great gal your way, one with a more sensitive, feminine heart.

A girl with a Christian heart should receive this discussion of the boundaries for what it is—a warm welcome to enjoy the adventure with you. When you state your standards openly, you're offering her the chance to be swept up in an adventure that is bigger than the both of you, as well as an opportunity to grow with God as never before. Carrie jumped at the chance, and she's having the time of her life:

> I was getting unhappy in my relationship with my boyfriend, Seth, because he just couldn't control his sexual passions around me, but *Every Young Man's Battle* changed my perspective on men completely, and I began to understand the huge struggle that guys face every single moment of their day. I had no idea that even the slightest little thing

could make a difference, like whether I wore a bulky sweatshirt or a fitted shirt. I began to realize that there were many things I could do to help Seth in this battle for purity. We began talking about this purity thing a lot, and I began to hold him accountable and to encourage and pray for him continuously.

Then Seth admitted he'd been struggling with porn on the Internet. Even though that was a breakthrough for us, I confessed that hearing about it hurt me tremendously, like he was cheating on me. After all, dating is a mini-marriage, as far as I'm concerned.

The good news is that we decided to attack this thing together. Now, whenever Seth has to go onto the Internet for anything, he calls me to let me know he's going online, and I pray for him until he calls back to let me know he's off the computer.

I know that both of us aren't perfect, but when I compare where we are today to where we were a few months ago, I see an absolute miracle of God. Seth and I are actually happy again, taking control of our problems together and learning to depend on God, which has made all the difference in the world.

I don't know if Carrie and Seth's "mini-marriage" will ever end up at a wedding altar, but if it doesn't, I know one thing for certain: by sharing his battle with Carrie early on, Seth has left her far better off for having known him. Their sweeping adventure has been a priceless internship for Carrie because she's learning how to trust God in prayer like never before, and she's learning how to be an awesome helper for her husband one day, an idea that's scriptural: "The LORD God said, 'It is not good for the man to be alone. I will make a helper suitable for him.'… For this reason a man will leave his father and mother and be united to his wife, and they will become one flesh" (Genesis 2:18, 24).

The word *helper* comes from a Hebrew word in Genesis that means "a help as his counterpart." So what does a helper do? In marriage, a wife's role is to help lift her husband—boost him, assist him, encourage him—to Christian greatness, whatever that may entail. In essence, it means that a wife will never allow her husband to drift to his lowest level. Instead, she'll help him be a godly man.

A girlfriend can play that same role in a dating relationship, and we ought to do everything we can to encourage our girlfriends to be our helpers too. A normal Christian girl will jump at the chance to help you. One of the deepest cries of her heart is to be swept up in a grand adventure with her hero as you chase God together, and she was literally created to be a helper and an influential responder in her romantic relationships with men.

That's why you shouldn't be slow to invite her onto purity's battlefield with you. Now, I still believe it's best for your accountability partners to be men, as I taught in *Every Young Man's Battle,* but at the same time, your girlfriend has her own distinct and vital role that she can play in your life because she's so near you. You need her help, and she'll love being part of a great quest with God. Amy has set her heart to get it done:

> After reading *Every Young Man's Battle,* I'm determined to help Brian be the man I know he ultimately wants to be every time he whispers, "Stop me if I'm going too far" or "Tell me if you're uncomfortable. Don't let me make you feel less valuable."
>
> That's his heart's conviction, and I want to make sure he finishes with that same conviction. I'm really committed to helping both of us share a pure relationship with each other and with God. For one thing, I've made a list of dates that we can go on to help us get to know each other better—dates that will also keep us in the public eye and safe from sexual temptation. My list includes going ice skating, making cookies in my kitchen (when at least one of my parents or three younger brothers will be around), and going to dinner and a movie with another couple we respect.
>
> I want to do all I can for him. Brian has all the qualities on my list for my future husband, but the truth is, we're still both single until our wedding day, and we're not there yet. If we don't end up married, I want to

leave him purer and better for the girl he does end up with. Am I on the right track?

Amy, I have three answers for you: Yes, yes, and yes!

Some authors will tell you not to talk about these issues, fearing an all-cards-on-the-table discussion about sexual matters might jump-start sexual activity, but that seems incredibly naive to me, especially when you consider the differences between guys and gals. Girls are different from us, and you will be a huge mystery to her. Without your guidance, she won't be able to help you because she won't even know when she's being inappropriate. You need to tell her, just like Jake did. Here's how that experience went for him:

I've been dating a wonderful Christian girl who is rock solid in her faith. Although we have set clear, defined boundaries—no kissing on the couch, no being in my apartment alone together—sometimes things still get out of hand, not to a terrible degree, but enough to where I feel we'd be stronger as a Christian couple if we could cut those things out of our relationship.

I have told her some things—like her low-cut shirts or kissing around the neck—can bring me down, but it can be awkward trying to cover everything that trips a guy's trigger. Would you recommend giving her *Every Young Man's Battle* to read so that she would better understand how guys work?

Absolutely. In fact, while she's reading *Every Young Man's Battle,* you should read *Every Young Woman's Battle* by Shannon Ethridge so that you can better understand what trips *her* triggers. She can't help you if she doesn't understand you, and if you don't ask her to read *Every Young Man's Battle* or this book, *Hero,* she'll likely keep doing the same old things that make you stumble. You can't afford that, so teach her. Again, that's part of being a hero, and that's part of leaving her better off for having known you.

From Jasen:

I stayed quick on the trigger in sharing with Rose what I felt our physical boundaries should be, and she was just as quick to chime in with her thoughts as well. We agreed early on that we shouldn't put our hands on each other's thighs, for instance, and that chest-to-chest hugs should be out of bounds.

It's not that Rose and I didn't touch each other at all when we were dating. We did decide that it was okay if we held hands, and we enjoyed that a lot. We also decided that it was okay for me to put my arm around her and do side hugs, but we were also careful that we didn't get too close or rub up against each other as we walked or sat close together.

I just think it's important to be careful where your arms and hands are so you don't bump into the wrong areas. You don't want to get your mind racing and end up back at your dorm room all fixated on her body.

Because Rose and I were careful, these things didn't happen too frequently. Consequently, I didn't have a lot of trouble keeping my mind in check. Of course, though we set our boundaries early, we couldn't predict all of the accidental touches that happened along the way, so we had to keep an ongoing discussion happening to prevent these from becoming an issue of lust for me.

One time, about two weeks after we started dating, we were holding hands and walking closely together through the skywalks in Des Moines. We were side by side for the most part, but she was leaning on me. Since this was early in our relationship, she was especially excited to be out with me, and she was kind of skipping along and bumping into me as we walked. While she wasn't doing anything on purpose, her chest brushed against me a number of times that night.

As I said, chest-to-chest hugs can get your engines going for obvious reasons, and believe me, as a red-blooded guy, I noticed when her breasts were brushing against me. I knew it would be easy for my mind to get racing lustfully, and I didn't want to go there.

As we walked romantically along the skyway, I figured Rose didn't know what was happening inside me. I certainly wasn't going to make a big deal out of it, but

I did want to mention it. I think we stopped for a treat or something, and I simply said, "You know, Rose, I think we have to be careful about how close we're walking next to each other. I think it would be better to keep just a little more distance between us. I don't want to make this a big deal, but bumping into your chest made me afraid that it would lead to something more in me, and I knew you wouldn't want that to happen."

Her reaction was classic, and something we all need to remember as men.

"Oh, Jasen. I'm so sorry. I was wondering if I was getting a little too close back there. I wasn't sure how men think or feel about things like that. I'm so glad you told me."

And then she said, "If you hadn't said anything, I would have just assumed you were fine with it."

Never be afraid to teach your girlfriend well. Most girls don't realize how little it takes to flip a guy's ignition switch, but the right girls will be glad you brought it up and made your needs clear. In my situation, had I said nothing about our "bumps" on the skywalk, Rose may have gone right on firing my engines—over and over again. Imagine trying to win your battle that way. But it wouldn't have been her fault. It would have been mine.

If you're going to remain pure during your dating relationships, you'll need to take the lead as a hero to set strong defenses and talk about them with your girl. We'll take a look at how to do that in the next chapter.

13

FLEEING

Stronghold Myth #8: A physical connection brings out the emotional connection. Setting boundaries on the physical inhibits your relationship from growing.

From Jasen:

If you believe this stronghold, you've been listening to too much popular psychology.

Without boundaries, your deepening emotional connection will only flow into a thick pool of sensuality, and if you've had any dating experience at all, you know that's true. You also know that dipping into that pool will *not* deepen your emotional connection but weaken it. If you want a healthy, deepening relationship with your girlfriend, you want boundaries.

Respecting boundaries is part of any healthy relationship, including your relationship with God. It's a sign of love and respect:

It is God's will that you should be sanctified: that you should avoid sexual immorality; that each of you should learn to control his own body in a way that is holy and honorable, not in passionate lust like the heathen, who do not know God.... Therefore, he who rejects this instruction does not reject man but God, who gives you his Holy Spirit. (1 Thessalonians 4:3–5, 8)

I didn't respect and follow God's standards of sexual purity as tightly as I did because I *had* to. I followed the standards tightly because I was under grace and I *wanted* to. That's what having a relationship is all about. Respecting boundaries is an act of love.

My highest priority in setting sexual defenses was the simple desire to obey God and protect His name and character, and that's what drove me to set good boundaries, even when I wasn't dating. But once I met Rose, I wanted real boundaries for a second loving reason. I knew that Rose had been hurt deeply by an earlier boyfriend, and I wasn't about to take risks with her heart, no matter how much the world said we needed to let our deepening emotional connection have room to grow. I didn't want to give myself away sexually to a cute girl and then break up, and I knew she couldn't take that either. Real men understand that true love requires true defenses.

Sure, wedding bells seemed to be chiming from the moment I met her, but I also knew that no guy can be 100 percent sure he'll end up marrying his girlfriend, no matter how loudly the bells gong. My dad said not to fall for his old excuse: *I'm going to marry her anyway, so why not jump into bed?*

Traditionally, Christian guys have done a poor job defending their girlfriends' purity, so I figured I'd have to ramp up my defenses above the traditional church standards of chastity and respecting the opposite sex.

Chastity simply doesn't go far enough. While I wasn't going to experience intercourse before marriage, there were also a lot of other things I *could* do and still remain technically a virgin. I didn't want to experience "everything but—" outside of marriage. As for respecting the opposite sex, that sounds good, but these days the term "respect" is nearly useless when it comes to setting up your defenses in a dating relationship. Remember one of the oldest come-on lines there is? "But I'll respect you in the morning."

Having said that, what does *respect* really mean? One thing I know is that it's way too easy to rationalize what respect means in the heat of the moment because you can be thinking, *I really respect her*, while doing something you'll regret. Besides, what if the girl you're with has no real boundaries of her own? There's not much there to respect, is there? You might feel like it's open season or like anything goes.

Without clean, practical defenses, it's way too easy to slide down the slippery slopes over and over again. For myself, I wanted practical defenses that Rose and I both understood and that I could easily apply to our relationship as the leader. Above all, I wanted to stay out of those hot moments entirely.

When it comes to setting up genuine practical defenses in *your* relationship, I suggest that you stop thinking about respecting the opposite sex and replace it with the phrase "flee bad situations." Remember, fleeing lines you up directly with God's wisdom on the matter: "Flee from sexual immorality. All other sins a man commits are outside his body, but he who sins sexually sins against his own body" (1 Corinthians 6:18).

But fleeing bad situations does far more than that too, because it deals practically and directly with the main culprit behind your sexual sin. The idea of respecting the opposite sex doesn't.

Think about it. In most cases, a guy doesn't blitz past a girl's boundaries because he's experienced a sudden, catastrophic drop in his respect quotient. No, most of the time it's because he's experienced a sudden rise in his body temperature.

From a practical perspective, he's intentionally or unintentionally put himself into a bad situation—like being alone together with no one around. Alone at her parents' place or her apartment, soon there's cuddling and kissing, then more touching, and wham! Before you know it, the engines are running so high into the red zone that lust takes over and blasts you off the tracks, like a runaway freight train.

Too late to flee sexual immorality.

That's why I chose the specific instruction of fleeing bad situations over the general idea of respecting women. You need to avoid the heat altogether and flee *before* you end up on the couch with her when no one else is around.

The truth is, we can all make mistakes, given the wrong situation.

It's fine and good to make a pact with your girlfriend to remain chaste and to respect each other at all times. But it's far better to agree that you won't spend any alone time together out of sight of others. That's where the real danger lies.

Here's how a family friend named Danny handled this "alone time" situation:

I set up some rules to keep me out of such situations as best I could. In practice, this meant that I was not to be alone with the person I was dating. Obviously, I didn't take this to the extreme. I could ride in a car with her, for instance. On the other hand, if we were sitting in the car talking, it had to be in a place like her parents' driveway—not some Lovers' Lane. I also made it a rule that I couldn't be alone in a house with the girl I was dating.

I kept these standards when I moved out and away from my parents because I felt it was wise and very honorable to God. Of course, it was much easier when I was living at home. I could say, "I can't do it because my parents won't let me." Now I had to keep those same standards as my own. But what a great standard!

I've just gotten married, and you better believe that I'm so glad that I stood strong, especially when Lisa and I were engaged. I can think of several occasions when, without this standard living strong in our lives, it would have been easy to lose the purity in our relationship.

Before we got married, Lisa and I allowed ourselves to sit in the car and talk many times in my parents' driveway. (While I no longer lived there, we often visited.) The neighbors would always peek out their kitchen curtains at us. We always waved at them, but we never got a wave in return! God bless those neighbors—they were definitely a part of our accountability, whether we liked it or not. I'm sure my mom was doing the same thing, but at least she was never obvious about it!

Before I met Rose, I never thought much about how dangerous it can be to your purity to spend time alone together with your girl. But once I started dating her, the dangers were instantly clear. It became obvious that the best way to avoid putting the two of us into bad positions was for me to lay out our boundaries as early in our relationship as possible.

We had a great discussion early on when it became apparent that, yes, something special was happening here. First off, we decided that we could only be alone together in public places. That meant, for instance, that we could be alone together in a park where people might walk by, or be alone together in restaurants, which are bustling with people. But we wouldn't allow ourselves to be alone in, say, the basement of our house, which is not a public place and where it would be unnatural for someone to happen by—unless your father is the author of *Every Man's Battle*. (Just kidding, Dad.)

Of course, the moment you set a boundary is the very moment the challenges to that boundary begin, but that's okay. Challenges simply give you another opportunity to stand up and lead like a man.

Ben faced an opportunity like this. "The idea of staying out in public makes a lot of sense to me. But what about doing stuff like mountain biking on backwoods trails or just chilling together with a hike around a mountain lake or in the forest? I love the outdoors. I completely agree that it wouldn't be a good idea to be all by ourselves in a house, since that could be asking for serious trouble. But I love the outdoors, and that's where I hang out and chill with my other friends. Why can't I do that with my girlfriend? I just want to be able to hang out one-on-one with her, like I do with my other friends. Is that okay, or is that risky?"

When it comes to challenges to your boundaries like this, discuss it with your girlfriend and make sure she agrees with you, and then take the proper precautions. Rose and I wouldn't have done what Ben's suggesting because we wanted to be one-on-one in the kind of public places where it was likely that others would be around, and we believe Ben's idea is a lot more risky to his purity than he realizes.

That said, there's no problem with any guy being alone with his girl in the great outdoors, as long as you both know what your boundaries are and you both understand that there's no one out there to hold you accountable. I'm only warning you to put up defenses. Defend your weak spots, but then go enjoy God and all He has created. Live life abundantly, but live within His pure standards. Go ahead and ride mountain bikes in the back hills. If it becomes a problem, though, stop. If not, have fun. In short, lead your relationship like a man.

GET CREATIVE

When challenges like these arise, however, don't be too quick to throw in the towel and make exceptions. You've got to be willing to take a stand and stick to your guns as you go through your dating period, because compromise is always the easiest thing to do. At those times, let your creativity take over.

One of those challenges popped up for Rose and me one weekend about five months before we were married. During that summer, I lived about two hours away from home in Cedar Rapids while working an internship at Rockwell Collins, an aerospace and defense company. Every weekend, I drove home to visit Rose. At the same time, my grandmother Gwen was terminally ill from cancer, and her life was being wrung through the last grinding months of an awful death. By the time she passed away in mid-June, my mom and dad were wasted from exhaustion.

On a spur of the moment, Dad decided the family needed to just get away and give Mom a break before dealing with Grandma's house and possessions. So he loaded up the car and packed everyone off to Florida for a week of rest and decompression. I couldn't go because of my internship, and as it so happened, Rose's family had just left on a weeklong camping trip too.

You can figure out the problem here.

When I hit town that weekend to meet Rose, both of our parents' houses were empty. We'd been planning to watch a favorite movie at one of our homes, but since both families had left town, that would mean we'd have to be alone in one of the houses. We had nowhere to go, or so it seemed. But that's when our creativity took over.

"I've got an idea," I said. "You know how our neighbors are always out in their yards working, and there are dozens of walkers going past our house every night on the sidewalk?"

"Yeah…?" she nodded quizzically.

"Well, how about we watch the movie in the garage? I can go in and move the television and DVD player out to the garage, and I can bring out an end table for the popcorn and pop. I noticed my dad took the bench seat out of the van last week. We can move that in front of the television as a couch. If we open the garage door and face the couch toward the street, our 'home theater' will be as public as any other theater. There will be plenty of people walking by! What do you think?"

"That's cool! Let's do it!" she said enthusiastically.

It was a little work to haul the television out to the garage, but it worked out great. We kept all the lights on, intentionally, so even after the sun disappeared, people walking by could still look in and see us.

We had a lot of fun laughing and waving at the folks on their evening strolls, and you should have seen some of the looks on their faces. The funniest face, though, belonged to my father the following weekend when he pulled the family van into the driveway, only to find Rose and me ensconced in a new theater where his parking space used to be.

Being creative isn't all that difficult if you stick to the *public places* rule. Most of your dates will involve doing fun things together in public places anyway, like going to the mall or sledding or roller skating. It can get tricky if you like to watch DVDs like we do, but even that shouldn't be too hard as long as your family is home and you don't shut yourself up in some bedroom or basement. We always watched our videos in the family room where plenty of Stoekers would be milling around.

We could have gone to an upstairs bedroom or the basement, but that would have made it feel like an intrusion—even with the door open—for anyone coming up or down the stairs. We never set ourselves up in a place where it would make someone feel funny to come our way. That was the easiest way to avoid temptation and not do anything physical with each other.

Best of all, most of the time we were still "alone" enough to make Rebecca and Michael sick to their stomachs when we romantically whispered and giggled in each other's ears, so it didn't crimp this guy's style too much. Even with these boundaries, you can still do all the fun things you want with a little romance on the side.

As we dated that summer, we found it awfully hard to be away from each other for a whole week at a time, but the two-hour drive each way would have made it difficult for either one of us to visit the other during the week for a date. Besides, if she'd driven to Cedar Rapids, there would have been no one to keep us accountable at my apartment if my roommate were gone.

So again, we got creative. We found a small college town halfway between us called Grinnell, and we set up a standing date there every Tuesday night. Since neither one of us lived there, there were no apartments with couches or bedrooms with beds to tempt us. The college provided a beautiful campus for walking and talking, and since there were a lot of students around, there were plenty of public places and restaurants to entertain a couple our age. Grinnell didn't allow us to put ourselves in bad positions, so it was a safe place to meet during the week.

"Seriously, No Kiss?"

We're often asked about our decision to hold off on kissing until marriage. That doesn't surprise me. It sounds extreme by today's standards. I certainly don't think it's a sin to kiss a girl before you're married—and neither does my dad. His guideline has always been fairly simple: never do anything with a girl you'd feel uncomfortable doing in front of her father.

Obviously, that could certainly include a kiss, but we decided on a tighter guideline.

Our decision not to kiss until our wedding day was really an extension of the *flee bad situations* philosophy. We didn't want to kiss until we were married simply because we thought kissing would make it harder to stay pure in the long run.

Obviously, you have to come to this decision together as a couple, and really, your girlfriend has to agree to it for *her* reasons and not just your own. If you make a unilateral decision and she's not kissing simply because you won't let her, she can get bitter, which can cause some real friction in the relationship.

I brought the idea up to Rose about a week into our budding relationship primarily because I figured that sooner or later, a couple begins to kiss to express their growing love for each other. But I also knew that kissing would be really exciting, and if things got exciting, I didn't know how our purity would stand up to it. I figured if I backed up the boundary all the way to no kissing, I'd be plenty safe.

And that was important to me because if the Enemy's work centered on tempting me to kiss Rose, even if I slipped up and kissed her, I'd still only be breaking one of *my* boundaries. God's standards would remain unbroken, and I'd remain pure in His eyes.

A lot of people push the line the other way, asking, *How far can I go without sinning? Where's the line? Can I touch you here? Can I go on to there?* But my line was backed up so far away from the danger zone that even if I blew it and kissed Rose, I wouldn't have compromised my walk with God.

Another reason I wanted to avoid kissing was because I didn't see how kissing would advance our relationship to any important degree. I once read somewhere that you can basically use your lips for one of two things—kissing or communicating. I suspected that our relationship might have a short dating and engagement period, so I thought our time would be better spent talking and getting to know each other really well.

Even if the two of you aren't moving quickly toward marriage, it's still really important to lay a good foundation of communication and get to know that person quickly so that if you don't fit together, you can move on before you get too emotionally attached to each other. You need to know who she is and what she believes, and you can learn a lot more by talking than by kissing. (I mean, "Duh!")

Anyway, since I thought it would be a good idea not to kiss in our relationship, I threw the suggestion out to Rose, and she was quite agreeable. "Hey, that's kind of what I wanted to do too," she said, and for us it was a done deal.

As we talked, I found that she had similar reasons to forgo kissing, but also a different one. She had been in a dating relationship where she did kiss, and then when they broke up, she felt so emotionally attached that the breakup was awful. She didn't want to put herself into that kind of pain again, so the idea of not kissing anyone else besides her husband resonated with her.

After making the decision to skip the kissing part, we talked about the other boundaries we wanted in our relationship. All this took place by the end of the first week that we were an item. All we had to do was move forward in unison after that.

Guys often ask me if all our boundaries were hard to keep. I don't think boundaries are ever super easy, but they weren't so bad during our dating time, especially during the time I was living in Cedar Rapids for the internship.

I will admit that things got a bit tougher during our four-month engagement. That's kind of weird because you'd think we'd have had a lot of experience defending our boundaries by then. The trouble was that the closer we got to our wedding day, the more we wrestled between two competing thoughts on the kissing front:

1. Well, in a few weeks we'll be married. Why not just go ahead and kiss now?

2. Don't kiss now! Why throw it all away now when we're this close?

Things got really bad for us two weeks before the marriage. In the grand scheme of things, you usually don't think of two weeks as very long, but if you're waiting to get married, it can seem like the longest time in the world. We both knew we would be disappointed later if we didn't wait to have our first kiss on our wedding day, so we held on. In other words, we couldn't relax our commitment as the wedding neared. We had to ramp it up.

And we're fortunate we did because we almost blew it. About a week before our wedding, I said, "Rose, how about if we just rub noses like the Eskimos and kind of sit and cuddle? I love you so much, and I just want to be close to you tonight."

Cuddling up and rubbing noses sounded fun to her, so we went ahead, with me rationalizing, *Hey, we're only a week away, and it isn't really kissing, so why not?*

We held each other close, and did the nose-to-nose thing and had some fun, but the alarm bells in my head just kept ringing louder and louder. Finally, I pulled away and said, "Rose, you know what? We're going to end up kissing here tonight if we don't stop this right now, and I don't want to rob us of that moment at the altar."

Ouch! She was not happy with me at that moment, and she did not enjoy having to stop.

But remember, when you face these moments, you're the man. You've got to take that stand to keep temptation at bay. Are you the hero or not? You have what it takes to come through at that moment if you'll just stand up and stick to your convictions, even if that temptation was all your idea in the first place.

In the end, we were both so glad our Eskimo kisses didn't lead us any further. We had an incredible wedding day, and our first kiss was awesome. Best of all, we had hundreds of people to enjoy it with us and nothing to regret on that day— or that night.

WARNING: OBSTACLES AHEAD

It pays to be careful about outside obstacles too. We were most tempted to back off our boundaries at my dorm room at Iowa State. I was in my last semester before graduation, and Rose and I had been engaged for a couple of months. Whenever Rose came to visit on campus, we'd keep my door open. In most places, that's no big deal, but in a college dorm, it can be extremely frustrating.

Loud drunks stumbling down the hall were bad enough, but an open door is an open invitation to anyone and everyone to come in and hang out. We would be continually interrupted by friends and acquaintances bopping in whenever Rose and I were sitting and talking. And three's a crowd, you know? And it was usually more like four or five or six, which meant that we never had any time to ourselves.

That was a frustrating time to keep the door open, but I knew I had no choice. Being all alone in a dorm room is not a bright move—especially when we were engaged. And my room was a single, so I didn't even have a roommate. We'd have been in an extremely tempting situation with that door shut.

But I'll tell you, one of the things that helped me strengthen my resolve was having a Christian friend who always left his door open during his engagement. Because of that example, I knew we could do it too, and that we weren't alone in this. I just had to be man enough to join him in it.

You're that kind of a man too. But even more, you aren't just a man, you're a chosen, gifted son of God. That's critical to realize if you want to overcome your biggest obstacle in this fight. When it comes to purity, don't just shrug your shoulders and say, "Hey, I'm only human."

You aren't only human. You're a son of the King! The apostle Paul chided the Corinthians for acting like mere men: "You are still worldly.... Are you not acting like mere men?" (1 Corinthians 3:3).

Paul was right. There's no excuse for acting like a mere man. You're His hero, His son. From the moment His spirit came into you, you lost all your rights to act like a mere man. It's time to step up when it comes to purity. Be the new creation you are. Don't just ladle the grace over your sin one more time. Stop sinning. Change.

Too many young Christian men believe they can live any way they like because grace will ward off every consequence of their sin. Why work so hard on their defenses? Grace will clean up the mess.

Yes, you do have grace—that's central to the gospel—but remember, willful sinning does nothing for your relationship with Him. Sinning drags you further apart from Him, which is the utmost of the bad positions you must flee while dating. Distance with God is devastating to your battle for purity because only a tighter relationship with the Father will help you stick to your boundaries.

At the end of the day, wherever you are on your spiritual journey, you want to move to a deeper and closer relationship with God. If you don't know how to do that, you need to read the second book in this series, *Tactics*. God wants to be close to you. He wants to take you into His confidence and to teach you how to be a man. He's simply waiting for you to turn to Him.

14

NO FEAR

Stronghold Myth #9: I'm afraid I won't be a good kisser when it counts, and what about the rest of my skills? If I don't practice beforehand, I'll embarrass myself on my wedding night.

From Fred:

Pop quiz: Name one guy you know who straggled back from his honeymoon shaking his head in shame and humiliation. I bet you can't.

I'm amazed at the things people say that have no basis in fact whatsoever. Megan, a college senior and friend of the family, told us that her college roommate was worried she'd "get in way over her head" on her wedding night.

What does that mean? *Way over her head?* Does it mean she'll crash her mental processors by taking in too much new information at once? Does it mean she won't be able to figure out how to hug and hold her heroic knight after dreaming passionately about this special and pure moment since she was a little girl?

That's ridiculous. It's Megan's roommate who's in over her head. She knows nothing about honeymoons.

Let me assure you: inexperience is not a bad thing on your wedding night. It's not like strapping on skis for the first time and riding a lift to the top of a black

double-diamond ski slope, or being handed a bat and told to go face the Cubs'
monster pitcher, Carlos Zambrano, with the World Series on the line at Wrigley
Field. Now *that's* being in over your head.

But sex? Come on! God didn't make it that hard, because the procreation of
the world is depending on it. Believe me, we're not talking rocket science here.
Having sex is about as tough as scratching your nose. You don't need a training
manual the first time around.

It makes no difference if you aren't Don Juan on your wedding night anyway.
I'm sorry to break it to you: the wedding night is rarely the pinnacle of sexual bliss
for any number of reasons, so don't build it up into something it was never
intended to be. If you're hoping for the best night ever on your wedding night, in
all likelihood, you'll be disappointed no matter how much practice you manage to
fit in beforehand.

Relax. Remember, the marriage bed is a wonderful place where you'll share
many long and glorious years exploring your hearts together. You needn't rush
things.

From Jasen:

If Rose and I appeared on *Larry King Live*, I'm sure he'd ask questions like:
*What was it like to have your very first kiss in front of so many people? What were
your thoughts as you approached that moment? Did you worry about looking
dumb?*

"Well, Larry, I was really looking forward to that first kiss, let me tell you. But
I'll have to admit I was a little worried about it early on because I hadn't kissed
anybody before and nobody wants to look like a dork in front of four hundred
friends."

My Uncle Brent had joked that we should buy a couple of doorknobs and
practice on those. Believe it or not, we actually did get the doorknobs, but we
never got around to taking them out of the package because we were so close to
the wedding that we figured it really didn't matter anyway. By the time we got to

the kissing part in the ceremony, I wasn't afraid at all, mostly because weddings are nuts! There had been so much genuine stress leading up to our wedding that by the time I got to the you-may-kiss-the-bride part, the nerves were long gone and I was ready to give it a shot.

I was glad, too, because as kisses go, that kiss went just about how I wanted it to. I mean, I gave her a big one, but the kiss was tastefully done, if I may say so myself. I'd been to a lot of weddings, and I'd seen some where the groom gives his newly minted bride the smallest peck, and you're like, *What was that?* I've been at other weddings where you end up squirming uncomfortably in your seat because the kiss was so long and sloppy. I wanted to land somewhere in the middle, something along the lines of a nice solid kiss that's not ridiculously long, but says, "I've waited a long time for this."

Our first kiss was perfect, and the crowd sure loved it.

Don't worry at all about holding back on the wonders of exploration until you're married. My dad once told me, "Jasen, throwing a football forty yards down the field and hitting a receiver in full stride is a lot harder than sex, and that takes a lot of practice for any young quarterback. But sex? That's the most natural thing in the world." Dad was right. I don't think I'll ever hit a receiver forty yards downfield, but Rose and I are doing just fine together. So believe me, this "early practice" thing is vastly overrated.

Our honeymoon was plenty soon enough to practice, and it'll be plenty soon for you too. If you want to work on your skills together, Rose and I recommend the book *Intended for Pleasure* by Ed Wheat. It's an older book, but a good one, and it isn't laced with shades of our pornographic culture found in some of today's Christian sex books. Just remember, you should avoid reading *any* of these books until after the wedding, as they'll get your imagination running too hot, and that simply isn't helpful to you in your battle for purity as a couple.

This "I'll embarrass myself on my wedding night because I won't know what I'm doing" business has never made much sense to me from the beginning. Practice beforehand? Come on! Sex is going to be fun no matter how late you start, and as for heavy practice, let me remind you that you're not playing for all-state honors here, and no one will be keeping score. Once, before our wedding, a guy asked me a question that's fairly typical of the American mind-set: "How will you know what you'll both like if you don't have sex before you get married?"

I was ready for him. "When you've been waiting as long as I have," I said, "believe me, you'll like anything."

Lighten up, guys! The wedding night is only a starting point anyway. You can always refine your tastes later as you enjoy the wonders of exploration with the love of your life. If you're open with each other and tell each other what you like or dislike, you will quickly learn to enjoy being together, and sex will get better every time, no matter where you start out. Best of all, you won't be like the "practiced" couples we've known who've cried on their wedding nights because they'd spent so much time on the practice fields that they had nothing left to share with each other that was special or new.

From Rose:

Guys seem to care a lot about how good at kissing they are, but girls don't really worry about that too much. If she finds you attractive but a bit inexperienced, she's not going to mock you. She'll think that's cute and, if she's normal, it will mean the world to her that you *haven't* been practicing on other girls.

Jasen's purity and inexperience has been one of the best things about our marriage, and I wouldn't want it any other way. I feel so confident knowing that I don't have to wonder if he's thinking about some other woman when we're together.

Jasen's inexperience was a wonderful gift to me on my wedding night. I felt so comfortable and free to be me. As a guy, you may not understand just how constantly girls are comparing themselves to other girls every day of the week, but because Jasen had been pure, he could offer me this one place of perfect security in my life where I knew I'd never be compared to another woman. What a gift— one that few women will ever receive from their husbands.

I've had people ask me, "How did sex change your relationship when you finally got there?" Well, it was a huge firecracker moment, no question about it. It was awesome. But did it change our relationship? Not really.

We were far more in awe of the fact that we had just made a covenant to each other in front of four hundred people and in front of God. That's the thing that left us breathless, and while sex came with that, it was the fact that we were finally married that meant the most to us.

That being said, we loved every minute of our first night together. I love surprises, and everything about it was an amazing surprise. We didn't know anything but the joy of getting to know each other, and the wonder of knowing that we both now knew a part of the other that nobody else in the whole world knows. That kind of surprise package beats them all.

If you think that only your practiced skills can bring on the thrills, I've got news for you. That isn't even remotely true. The anticipation of doing something new together for the first time had been building for months, and that, too, added immeasurably to the thrill. You start dating, you get engaged, you walk up to the altar, you exchange vows, you have that first kiss, you go to the reception, you get in the limo, and before you know it, you're standing in the honeymoon suite alone together. What a crazy, precious moment you'll remember for the rest of your life!

Let me return for a moment to that first kiss at the altar. Having our lips touch for the first time was so priceless and so worth the wait, and it was awesome hearing everyone scream and cheer for us. After all of the lonely nights and all of the dreamy journal entries and all of the edgy days waiting for Jasen to finally begin pursuing me, I couldn't believe my dreams had come true and that I was finally in his arms. He was mine, completely mine. No amount of practice could deliver these kinds of thrills.

Nor can it deliver the kind of balance we have in our relationship. Sex never dominated our relationship before the wedding, and sex has never dominated our relationship *after* the wedding, even though it's awesome. Jasen is the prize, not his body, and I know he feels the same way about me. I'm absolutely certain that God intended our marriage to be that way and He wants that for every marriage.

The discipline of waiting revealed a lot about our love for each other. For one thing, our love isn't shallow. We've known a lot of people who won't date someone unless they know they can have sex pretty soon after they're an item. I knew that wasn't the case with Jasen, and he knew that wasn't the case with me. That sure made dating uncomplicated.

The way we did things also set us up for a lifetime of trusting each other. He had such self-control during our dating days that I know that if he's ever out of town on a business trip, this thought will never cross my mind: *What's he doing in his hotel room when he's there alone without me?*

I know a ton of women who worry about that, but I'll never have to. Even when he's at work with other women, I know our relationship is safe. His discipline has proven that he loves me, and that I'm not just about sex to him. For him, it's always been about our relationship and about understanding my heart and what makes me who I am. *That's* a thrill to a woman. I don't care how good you think your practice has made you in bed. If you've spent a lot of time practicing on women, you'll never be able to offer this kind of thrill to your bride. Sexual thrills aren't the only kind of thrills that a woman desires, and only pure heroes can deliver *this* kind.

From Jasen:

Instead of worrying about whether or not you'll embarrass yourself on your wedding night, perhaps it's time to worry about something else, especially in light of the other stronghold myths we've taken to task in the last nine chapters: *Do you believe God?* Have you ever really put anything costly on the line in your stand for your faith?

Some men truly believe God. Others merely believe *in* Him. There's a vast difference between the two. God has made promises that He'll bless the obedient. Do you really believe that God will give you all of the same things Rose and I have received if you put His kingdom first and tear down the strongholds of thinking in your life? You now have the opportunity to lay some things on the line to see if it'll happen.

If you believe God, of course, you're already waiting for the proper time to experience your sexuality in order to protect her and to defend His ways and His character.

If you haven't, you've laid nothing on the line for your faith, and perhaps you don't believe God as much as a son ought to believe Him. Consider for a moment these words from the apostle Peter: "Dear friends, this is now my second letter to you. I have written both of them as reminders to stimulate you to wholesome thinking" (2 Peter 3:1).

This has been *my* goal in writing to you too. Our culture is so messed up that it's difficult to know the wholesome from the common these days, but God's Word is always wholesome, always urging us to live a life worthy of sons (Ephesians 4:1). On the other hand, the stronghold myths we've laid out in this book are unwholesome and urge us to live unworthy lives before Him.

Wherever you fall between the extremes, by this point of the book your mind has been challenged by the uncommon ways God has called each of us to think and to live by, and perhaps you've discovered some unwholesome ways of thinking in you. If so, God has a plan for you to engage with Him: "We demolish arguments and every pretension that sets itself up against the knowledge of God, and we take captive every thought to make it obedient to Christ" (2 Corinthians 10:5).

God's Word is a test to the wholesomeness of your thinking, and so, as we close this chapter, I'd like to give the Lord the last word regarding the strongholds in your life and to give Him a chance to stimulate some wholesome thinking in you. First, meditate on each verse of Scripture for a moment, and then ask yourself the questions that follow:

"Remember your leaders, who spoke the word of God to you. Consider the outcome of their way of life and imitate their faith" (Hebrews 13:7). *Have you considered the outcome of your current way of life with girls? Is it worthy to be imitated from God's perspective?*

"Pray for us. We are sure that we have a clear conscience and desire to live honorably in every way" (Hebrews 13:18). *Do you have a clear conscience when it comes to the girls in your life? Do you desire to live honorably in every way?*

"This is how we know that we love the children of God: by loving God and carrying out his commands. This is love for God: to obey his commands. And his commands are not burdensome, for everyone born of God overcomes the world. This is the victory that has overcome the world, even our faith" (1 John 5:2–4). *You say you love your girlfriend. Are you obeying God's commands regarding purity when you are with her? If not, you don't genuinely love her. You love yourself.*

"He who heeds discipline shows the way to life, but whoever ignores correction leads others astray" (Proverbs 10:17). *Will you heed discipline or will you lead your girlfriend astray?*

"The righteousness of the upright delivers them, but the unfaithful are trapped by evil desires" (Proverbs 11:6). *Are you demanding to be delivered by grace instead of by your own right choices?*

"I guide you in the way of wisdom and lead you along straight paths. When you walk, your steps will not be hampered; when you run, you will not stumble. Hold on to instruction, do not let it go; guard it well, for it is your life" (Proverbs 4:11–13). *Do you hold on to God's instructions regarding your sexual relationship with your girlfriend as if your life depended upon it? If so, give some examples.*

"For the LORD takes delight in his people; he crowns the humble with salvation. Let the saints rejoice in this honor and sing for joy on their beds. May the praise of God be in their mouths and a double-edged sword in their hands" (Psalm 149:4–6). *Have you joyfully accepted God's call to purity as a single man, singing His praises night and day while wielding the double-edged sword of His Word in fighting for the honor of His girls? Are you honored to be His warrior in this battle or are you frustrated with Him?*

Gratefully, God will continue to call out our manhood by confronting our will for as long as we live, and He's done it one more time with this test. As you begin to tear down whatever strongholds of thought you have in your life, I'd like to encourage you by sharing some final testimonies of other Christian men who chose to step up as heroes in this world.

15

DO HARD THINGS

This e-mail came to my dad:

> I've been pure for the last 131 days. The Word of the Lord has been my
> strongest tool in overcoming any temptations, and His wisdom has pierced
> the Enemy. I'm twenty-four years old, single, and mature enough to let go
> of my past. I'm looking forward to continuing in my purity and seeing
> what God has planned for my life. I'm grateful to the Lord and proud of
> myself for following this pathway to victory, especially because I live on my
> own, without family or roommates to hold me accountable. I'm happy to
> report that I'm exercising self-control by the power of God, and I know
> that one day my marriage will be a lot more fruitful because I've learned
> this.

As men, one of our greatest weaknesses is our tendency to stay silent about our
sexuality. When we do, it gives our common enemy his greatest advantage. Traps
remain hidden, and the men walking behind us fall in when they could have so
easily avoided them. We miss out on the cheers of encouragement that could
inspire even greater victories. And we forfeit the tighter bond that comes from
sharing life's journey together.

I understand it, but I don't like it. I've been the same way, not wanting to put
myself out there for fear of embarrassment or saying something wrong. But when

you stand up and share your testimony that first time, like I did at Glen Eyrie, it's like the dam doors open up and people start responding.

There's just a natural power in an authentic testimony. My story's been broadcast nationwide in the UK, and now I'm writing this book with my dad. It's crazy to think how far it's gone, but now I have no question about how important others' stories are to our strength as Christian men.

Like many people, I used to think testimonies were filler material to add a little interest and round out a message, like the salt and pepper on a plate of baked chicken and dumplings. But now I believe a good testimony is just as important as the teaching because of what it can do for your faith. Testimonies *are* the chicken and dumplings; they are a powerful thing, as we mentioned in the introduction. My dad says what gave him the courage and the faith to step out in such radical obedience to God was the testimony in Job 31:1 where Job makes this startling revelation: "I made a covenant with my eyes not to look lustfully at a girl." And the reason we know it worked for him can be found in the beginning of the book: "In the land of Uz there lived a man whose name was Job. This man was blameless and upright; he feared God and shunned evil" (Job 1:1).

Job didn't just make that covenant, he kept it! The most transforming part of that verse for my dad was that Job was just an ordinary man. He thought, *If he can do it, so can I.* Job's testimony gave Dad courage and faith to believe God could do it again in his life.

Testimonies build your faith and guard your commitment. That's why we want to share some with you in this chapter.

Do you know what happens when we stop talking about God's work in our lives? When things get tough, we're often left in fear and unbelief, just like the Israelites who frequently forgot to consult the record books of the things God had done for them. Whenever they quit talking about what God had done in the past, they ended up rebelling and sinning, instead of believing that God could "do it again" for them in the present.

Consider what God did in Kellen's life:

I'm twenty-one and in the military, and I have always considered myself a man's man. Somewhere along the line, though, I had rationalized in my pride that I could be a man's man and a God's man at the same time. It wasn't hard to make that mistake.

I grew up in church and have been born again for as long as I can remember and have always had a desire for God's will in my life. I traveled a lot when I was young, and that's how I first discovered pornography. Oddly enough, I was in Tahiti, innocently wandering the grocery store when I stumbled across a stash of porn magazines openly displayed in unwrapped packages. I was shocked but also fascinated, and over time I became more and more heavily entrenched in porn. For years I tried to fight it, but more recently I just gave up and slid headfirst down into the pit. By the time I hit bottom, I was so frustrated and tired of the battle that I was thinking, *I'm either going to stop living in this sin, or I'm going to go out and start having sex with every woman I can find, starting with prostitutes.*

Finally, something changed. I came to a critical point of decision. In desperation, I prayed, "Will you help me with this sin, Lord? It's got to go, but I don't know how to stop it!" I remember clear as day when I heard about your book, *Every Man's Battle*, shortly after that prayer. I was in church reading the bulletin when I saw this line: "Every Man's Battle— a six-week study that starts tonight at seven o'clock."

God nudged me hard. I approached the individual teaching the class and told him I was interested. He was seventy-six years old and well known as a man of God. He asked me my age, and then he looked me square in the eyes and said directly, "You need this, Son."

I sure wasn't arguing. I bought the book, read it in two days, and haven't looked at porn in six weeks. But even more importantly, I have repented of my sins, made a covenant with my eyes, and strive daily to bounce my eyes. I began memorizing Scripture, and my time in the Word each day became alive again. I actually pray and talk with God now.

Of course, I'm no Pollyanna. I'm still in a real battle, but now I have a sword and a shield, and I am prepared to fight till the death. Imagine! Less than two months ago I was ready to pay someone to take my virginity from me. Today, I stand ready to defend my sexual purity with my life, and not just mine, but that of my brothers and sisters in Christ around me as well. I'm a man now, and things will never be the same. Thanks for giving my manhood back to me.

This sentence from Kellen's e-mail stood out to me: "Finally, something changed. I came to a critical point of decision." Kellen finally found his battle to fight, and now he's brandishing the sword and shield that every true knight of the cross is called to bear. He was made for this, and his heart is now fully alive and kicking.

As sons of God, we've been given this sensual world to conquer and the women in this world to defend. I don't know about you, but Kellen is having the time of his life.

And he's not the only one:

G'day! My name is Mick, and I live in New Zealand. I am twenty years old and have been a Christian for as long as I can remember. I was amped to finally find a book that confronted pornography and sexual impurity head on. I am passionate about seeing our society wake up to this lie that the devil has told us, so good on you for writing this book. Top man!

Toward the end of last year, my friendship with Stephanie started to move toward being more than friends. But I knew it could never be until I dealt with my porn problem, as I was *not* going to take this habit into the relationship and hurt her as well.

She came down to stay at my parents' for a couple of days, and during this time we talked about our relationship. I told her that I wanted to ask her out, but I felt God was telling me that now was not the right time. She agreed, as she felt the same way. After she left, I sensed God telling me that I could only ask her out after six months of being porn-free.

Game on. At the end of each day, I put up a drawing pin into a corkboard to signify that I hadn't looked at porn that day. At the end of the week, I attached a square of paper, and at then end of each month, I put up a little card. I kept in contact with Stephanie regularly during the six months, but we kept everything purely on a friendship basis.

I am happy to say that I completed my time without breaking my contract with God, and I sensed a release from the Lord to ask her out. We've been having a blast dating each other. Heaps of fun! I really appreciate her after having to wait, and this discipline will really help me out in our relationship.

You see, one of Steph's love languages is physical touch, which means I'll need to be the strong one in the relationship. We made the rule that we wouldn't kiss each other because I wasn't willing to take such a risk with her purity, especially considering that kissing can quickly lead to other things. I want to go after God, and that means I need to continue defending her purity just as fiercely as God was defending it when He asked me to wait six months. I want to be a man after God's own heart.

Don't you just love it when someone gets it? Mick's adventure inspires us in our own. Seeking purity is about more than being obedient. It's about more than becoming a nice guy. It's about rising up as a warrior of God and standing for Him, come what may.

God called Mick to do something very difficult, and he did it. And his example helps to confirm that ruling and subduing our sexuality is simply part of being a man.

A Time of Testing

It's time for our generation to rebel sexually and change the face of manhood all over the world. In 2 Timothy 2:22, Paul instructs us to "flee youthful passions and pursue righteousness, faith, love, and peace, along with those who call on the Lord from a pure heart" (ESV). Nineteen-year-old twins Brett and Alex Harris, authors of *Do Hard Things,* believe that this verse "captures the rebelutionary mind-set of collaboration: rebelling against low expectations ('flee youthful passions'), doing hard things ('pursue [or strive after]'), and harnessing the power of teamwork ('along with those who call upon the Lord from a pure heart')."[1]

There is no harder thing than remaining sexually pure before marriage, and there is no other place where our selfless, countercultural collaboration with our brothers will be more effective in impacting our culture as a generation.

Imagine all our stories coming together and serving to embolden and empower those around us who haven't yet realized the freedom and joy in accepting this truest mark of manhood.

From Fred:

I can't possibly agree more with Brett and Alex's premise here. The battle God calls us to is one of collaboration, or fighting together for the same cause—purity in our world, in our time.

But you haven't just been given a battle to fight and some damsels to save. You have brothers out there, as well, and you're to fight *for* them and win *with* them, together in arms. You can start with the brothers living closest to you—those in your own home.

Kevin wrote to tell me that he stepped up to fight for his brother's destiny:

Every Young Man's Battle and *Tactics* have made huge impacts on my life. For a long time, I knew what I needed to change, I just couldn't figure out where to start. Your books led me on that journey I needed to take, and I'll never regret the effort it took.

But this isn't really about me. You see, I'm a senior in high school, so I'll be leaving for college next year. But I have a brother in ninth grade, and unfortunately my dad has never been too big on the father-son talks. Although my mom has tried to talk to Ben, she can't really help him in the way another guy can. Since I don't want my brother to struggle like I did,

I must give him some direction before I leave for college. Where do I begin?

My spine tingled as I read his letter, and my heart soared. *A brother helping a brother! What a fantastic example of a man!*

I responded that he should pick up *Preparing Your Son for Every Man's Battle* and read the parents' section, "For Dad (or Single Mom)," at the beginning of the book. Then he could go through the other two sections with his brother.

A few months later, I received this e-mail:

Dear Fred,

I took a couple days reading through the Parent's Section and got the idea. After two weeks of getting up my courage, I talked to Ben who, as far as I knew, hadn't yet really started heading in the same direction of sexual sin that I had. We opened the book to the father-son chapters and read a ways, and then we talked about what we read for a little while.

I told him about what I was trying to do for him and began sharing some stories from my past. I was surprised. It wasn't really as awkward as I thought it would be. In fact, he seemed very interested in what I had to say, especially about my own stories. What I'd planned to be a twenty-minute discussion ended up being a three-hour hike around the lake in our neighborhood. I don't know how many laps we ended up taking that night!

At about the two-hour mark, I began sharing my thoughts about the differences between a "man's man" and a "God's man." Right about then, he stopped me and said, "You know, Kevin, at first I thought Mom put you up to this, but now I know it was your idea. I'm really glad you decided to talk with me."

Over the next month or so, we didn't keep a regular schedule on the reading, but we went on walks throughout the neighborhood every two weeks or so. We talked about bouncing the eyes and lots of your other principles as well. Ben was especially interested in my failed relationship attempts, which turned into a lot of good laughs together. Anyway, things turned out just like you said. My brother and I have become closer in the last few months than we've ever been our whole lives. I'm proud to be such an influence on his life.

Kevin is my hero, and I told him so. This is the kind of example we need more of, to encourage us to fight for our brothers—in our youth groups, in campus ministries, and in men's groups at church. It's always easier said than done—even youth groups can be warped and scarred by the spirit of Baal—but together we can overcome. It's so worth the effort, as you can see.

From Jasen:

My church youth group was very similar to my middle school and high school. A lot of the guys and girls who were popular at my school came to my youth group and remained popular there. The situation wasn't entirely the same because there were a number of people from different schools, but the cliques and social ladders were as strong at church as they were at school.

Ironically, the one big difference was that it was a *lot* more difficult to stand up for purity at my youth group than it was in my public school. Regarding movies, music, or other influences that could lower my standards, the peer pressure was far more intense from the Christian guys and girls. I remember a few guys who outright condemned me because I wouldn't watch a PG-13 movie at their house. I'd say, "Look, I don't want to look at naked people on the screen. To me, that's wrong."

That didn't play well with the youth-group guys. Most of them got angry. "Are you saying I'm not a Christian? I'm as much a Christian as you are!" A couple others said, "I watched it and I'm fine—so what's *your* problem?"

I never heard such comments at school. Sure, I'd get teased in the hallways from time to time, but most people let me off the hook. Not so in my youth group. They thought I was judgmental and out to make them feel guilty. They wouldn't even consider my position. The worst part—like a kick in the teeth—was how the Johnston High kids from my youth group totally ignored me between classes at school. And I was supposedly their Christian brother.

That was tough, but God gave me the proper response:

My dear friends, if you know people who have wandered off from God's truth, don't write them off. Go after them. Get them back and you will have rescued precious lives from destruction and prevented an epidemic of wandering away from God. (James 5:19–20, MSG)

I went after these guys by never backing down. That's the approach Jake Perkins, a youth pastor at the Edmond Church of Christ in Edmond, Oklahoma, took when facing the battle with his youth group. He knew he had to do something to help them:

Our youth ministry began a journey a few years ago. Little did we know the path before us would be filled with challenges, defeats, disappoint-ments, and heartbreak. But what we also didn't know was that those challenges and defeats would lead us toward a new hope in God's plan for purity—or that the veil would be torn away, sin would be exposed, and our youth group would be revolutionized to seek after God's standards. This is our story:

Dan, my youth volunteer, recommended the book *Every Young Man's Battle*. Once we'd read it, we were convinced that this was not your typical "pledge not to have sex" book. This was more of a call to manhood. Dan and I both wished someone had taught us this material when we were teens!

Still, the first five weeks were a struggle. The guys wouldn't talk, and the only difference between this study and any other study we'd done was that our guys were hearing words that they'd never heard in church before—words like *masturbation*. Dan and I were being as open and honest as we could about our own struggles, but nothing we said triggered anything from the guys in return.

Finally, on a van ride one afternoon, I got two of the guys alone and asked them what they thought about the class. After a little prodding, one of the guys, James, finally admitted, "Sure, I struggle with lust and masturbation every day. It is just so hard to talk about in front of other guys."

I pounced on that. "James, just say that in class this next week. Nothing more, nothing less. Can you do that?"

James could, and when he got real, the floodgates were opened. Within three weeks, every last one had spoken up and shared at least once, and our guys started to expose the sin for what it was and what it did to their lives.

The key to all studies, devotionals, and one-on-one talks is openness. Ephesians 5:11 says, "Have nothing to do with the fruitless deeds of darkness, but rather expose them." Whenever we shine the light of Jesus on the dark places in our lives, it's not shameful at all. Actually, it's absolutely freeing because we begin to live the way we're supposed to live.

When you're freed up, natural creativeness can blossom, and we saw that happen in spades. The guys created their own code language so they could check up on each other when others were around. For example, saying "How's your battle?" meant "Did you masturbate this week?" They also shook their heads in a certain way as a signal to remember to bounce the eyes.

Taylor used the forty days of Lent to do a television fast. During the six-week period, he realized how much television had been controlling his sex drive. Brandon began calling a different friend every day to check on his battle, which, in turn, helped him stay away from porn himself. JT began checking out trustworthy movie reviews online before going to see them in the theater. Jesse told me, "Now when we go to the movies together and a scene comes on that we know we don't want to see, we always catch each other and stare each other right in the face until the scene is over."

Our youth group took on a life of its own, and a new culture was formed. We soon set up accountability groups, and for three years we haven't looked back. Every guy, whether new to the group or not, now knows there are sexual and spiritual expectations in our group.

Our youth group is co-ed, of course, so at some point it became clear that we had to share these expectations with our girls. We put our heads together and came up with a plan. One Sunday morning, we separated the youth group by gender and had four girls share some of their struggles with the guys. Likewise, we had four guys share with the girls.

Our guys were speaking plain vanilla until Tim stepped up to the plate. He simply said, "Girls, some of the things you wear, even on Sunday mornings, make us lust and sometimes masturbate afterward."

You could hear a hairpin drop in that room. Tim had been straightforward, shocking, and honest, but it was also the truth. Because of what he said that morning, it's been two years since I have had to ask a girl to go home and change her clothes because she was dressed inappropriately.

A turning point happened the following spring for our men's group, which meets every Wednesday night. Thirty men were studying and talking about *Every Man's Battle*, but they were struggling to be as honest and upfront about the issues they were facing. After a couple months, the men's study group leader asked Dan and me to teach a couple of classes for them. On the first evening, during some back-and-forth with the men, we quickly learned they hadn't even used the word *masturbation* in their class, nor had they addressed the problem of pornography—after ten weeks of meeting together!

We knew exactly what to do. The following week, we brought along three of our teenage guys. As the Spirit began to move that night, all three of these guys heroically shared their struggles with lust and masturbation, right out loud and with their dads in the room. While their fathers were shocked by the honesty, nothing they said was out of line either. It was simple truth telling, shining the light of Christ on our sin.

What happened that evening was huge. Sin was exposed, and best of all, no father in the room had any excuse to avoid talking to their boys about their sexuality. I had never seen anything like it. Many of those dads are still talking about the battle regularly with their teens because of that one Wednesday night.

Jake's story is a vivid reminder that the battle is being won in many lives in many communities around the country. That's why I'm so optimistic that our generation—the one that arrived after the sexual revolution of the '60s—can be victorious. Today, men are finally talking about areas of our lives nobody has *ever* talked about—how our sexualized culture causes so many to get caught up in lust and lose their impact for the kingdom.

That's a really good thing, and I'm proud to be a part of it. And it's something we can all be proud of as we tell everyone what God is doing in our lives.

So don't back down from playing your part in the story God intends for you—or from sharing it again and again.

16

HOW TO LIVE

From Jasen:

I believe our generation is ready to rethink what we're capable of doing as men, especially in our sexuality. My grandfather's generation, as well as my father's, was quickly swept away by the sexual revolution that started in the '50s and '60s. Will our generation—the Millennials—be swept up in a revolution against the culture's deference to Baal and his "anything goes" mind-set?

Will we rebel against the conventional wisdom that premarital sex is expected? Will we rebel against the ideas that we have a First Amendment right to look at pornography or that it's perfectly okay to have children without getting married first? I've thoroughly enjoyed being a rebel, swimming against the cultural tide of sex-sex-sex 24/7.

John Eldredge agrees:

If we can reawaken that fierce quality in a man, hook it up to a higher purpose, release the warrior within, then the boy can grow up and become truly masculine.... The *real* you is on the side of God against the false self.... Your flesh is your *false self*—the poser, manifest in cowardice and self-preservation—and the only way to deal with it is to crucify it...shoot the traitor. How? Choose against him every time you see him raise his ugly head.[1]

It's about time we separate the men from the boys around here. What part will *you* play in this great cosmic war? Will you be a poser, or will you shoot the traitor and follow that deep desire for battle and adventure and beauty?

Look, there is a time in life to live heroically, and this is your time. Remember *The Lion King*? If you're anything like me, you've seen that movie at least a couple of times. Simba runs off and refuses to accept his responsibility as a young leader, instead taking up a life of ease in the jungle. *Hakuna matata.*

But later, upon hearing of his Uncle Scar's scandalous leadership, he runs back to find his former home destroyed. Had he stayed, he certainly would have been killed by Scar and his cronies. But once he'd matured and grown into his abilities, he was able to return and take up the battle.

These may not be the last days of human history, but without revival, our country's spiritual landscape will soon be as lifeless and desolate as Simba's home. But think about how Simba turned things around. He surveyed the ashen landscape. He rose to the challenge and fought, fulfilling his responsibilities. That's what men do.

As Simba stood with his friends on the edge of their destiny, he knew his courage over the next few moments would determine the course of their history for years to come. Simba came through.

This could be your moment. Will you come through?

Each of us is living at a key moment in history, poised on the edge of our destiny as young men. We have given ourselves over to Baal worship as a nation and opened the door to judgment, but God has opened a window of opportunity to divorce Baal and make another covenant with God.

I said it earlier, and I'll say it again: the damage to our culture caused by Christian men waiting too long to step into manhood has been devastating. And like Simba, we have a second chance to shoulder this responsibility. We have a birthright, and God is calling us to move out and mobilize.

Brett and Alex Harris posed serious, exciting questions to our generation in their book, *Do Hard Things*:

Could it be teenagers today are faced with a unique opportunity to do hard things—not just as individuals, but as a generation? And not just any hard things but big, history-shaping ones?… What is possible when a generation stops assuming that someone else will take care of the brokenness in the world—or that someone else will capitalize on current opportunities—and realizes that they are called to take action?[2]

The conventional wisdom claims that great quests are lived out by great people, but I don't think that's true. The small decisions we make every day define who we are and the world around us. I believe there's an essential importance to small decisions because it's the small decisions—done well—that define greatness.

Destinies are built upon small decisions, like the time I picked up my backpack and asked the teacher if I could hang out in the hall while a PG-13 movie played, or the time I moved the couch and television into the garage while my family was away on vacation. The small stuff matters, as they say, and every day there will be small decisions you must handle heroically—decisions that affect your destiny and the destinies of those around you. Never forget that the great quests are mostly lived out in the small decisions in the quiet corners of your life that no one sees.

Equipping Yourself for the Future

My younger brother, Michael, recently opted out of the sex education curriculum at the high school because it was all about how to put on condoms correctly, what diseased genitalia looks like, and other things like that. And some of the guys in the hallway got on his case.

"Don't be stupid, Michael," they said. "When you get to college, you won't know what you're doing, and you'll get your girlfriend pregnant or into some other kind of trouble."

It never occurred to these guys that he might be planning to go through college *without* going to bed with someone. But who decided that the only defense against screwing up your life is to equip yourself with condoms?

My brother *has* equipped himself, but he's riding toward a distant spot on a rugged frontier with a courageous girl in mind who'll join him in his quest for purity. Until then, he's willing to ride alone on that long, twisting trail, come what may. How many will join him?

There's an adventure out there waiting for you, an adventure with your name on it. Don't waste your single years. Rebel, like Michael has. Mount up and ride. Charge out and pick a fight with the enemy.

From Fred:

We are living in a critical time. What is good is bad, and what is bad is now good. As wickedness has increased, our love for God has grown cold, and few are willing to embrace social pain for His sake anymore, sexually or otherwise.

Sure, times are dark. Are these the last days of human history? I don't have an answer, but I do know one thing: these are certainly the last days of *your* history. You only get one life. How are you going to live it?

You don't know what tomorrow will bring or how much time you'll have. Let me share a story I told in *Every Man's Challenge.*

When a dim November sun peeked over the chilly horizon one morning, I rolled out of bed to shower and shave just like any other morning. I had no idea what lay ahead that day.

That afternoon, the air was crisp and a sparkling blue sky arched over Iowa, and I was tooling along West Des Moines' Eighth Street to deliver a package to a client. For some forgotten reason, I was driving Brenda's midnight blue Chevy station wagon that day, the one with the country squire wood panels. Definitely not a cool ride, but it was the finest car *I'd* ever owned, so humor me.

As with any guy driving a great car on a gorgeous afternoon, everything seemed right in the world. Business was good, and my third child, Rebecca, had just been born two weeks earlier. She was the cutest little Gerber baby on the planet.

Heading south, I approached a familiar intersection: Quality Ford on the left and Jimmy's American Café on the right. I glanced down at the speedometer—thirty-five mph—perfect, right on the nose. Things were smooth as a quiet lake on a sweltering midsummer eve.

Suddenly, a brand-new full-sized pickup—coming my direction—swerved out of his lane and into my path. Everything happened in a flash as we collided head-on. My right foot hit the brake at the instant of impact, locking my knee just in time for the full jamming impact. My shoulder strap failed to catch, and as my upper body flew forward, my left thumb caught the steering wheel, cracking the bone and snapping the ligaments that held it in place. My chest slammed into the steering wheel, which folded like a cheap accordion against the dash. The impact was equivalent to hitting a brick wall at sixty-five miles per hour.

I slumped back against my seat in a stunned, listless daze. Within seconds, it seemed, I heard sirens whine in the distance. I was amazed at the superhuman response time. "Man, these guys are good," I said to myself.

The light began to fade to gray, and my spirit began to slip away. I felt the moorings of my soul letting go, like the ropes of a great ship loosening and slipping from the pilings of the dock. Everything was so peaceful, so easy, so natural. I remember feeling quite surprised that I felt no trace of doubt. I knew exactly where I was heading—to heaven—and I had no fear. Rolling my head back in that peaceful moment, I remember thinking, *Death isn't such a big deal at all. It's kind of nice.*

But then, for no apparent reason, my spirit cried out in a stream of consciousness. I began to pray, *Lord, I want to raise my kids for You and make sure they are okay. They are so young, and I have so much to teach them. I want so badly to know them, and I love Brenda, and she'll be so alone, and now that we have everything working between us, I want to know her and love her and be the husband You wanted me to be.*

Suddenly, my spirit was frozen. Emotional electricity pierced through my core as my spirit realized the truth and cried, *Lord, I've done nothing for You yet. I have to stay here and do something for You.*

The intensity of my desperation rapidly kicked its way into the red zone as my spirit screamed, *Please, Lord, I want to live! I can't come to heaven empty-handed with nothing to give You. Look at all You've done for me! I really want to see You, but I can't come to You like this. Please give me a chance to get You something.*

Don't bring me to heaven empty-handed. Please let me live. I've got to have something to lay at Your feet.

As quickly as they had begun to slip, the moorings began to tighten back up again. A new and different peace now settled in over me. Having long ago memorized a number of hymns during my battle for sexual purity, I now began to praise Him, softly singing hymns in worship.

A female paramedic ripped the door open and, surveying the scene, knew there was no time to lose. She later said that with one look, she *knew* I'd never make it to the hospital alive. She'd seen this same situation many times before. My face was ashen gray from the massive internal bleeding in my chest cavity. A check of my blood pressure in the ambulance did nothing to dissuade her. She and other paramedics worked frantically as we sped away, and I heard her call ahead to prepare the trauma surgeons. They would have to open my chest immediately upon our arrival at the hospital.

I simply lay singing hymns softly under my breath and in total peace. The paramedics quickly rolled me into the emergency room. A witness had called Brenda from the accident scene, so she arrived about the same time I did. A chaplain met her at the door...the same chaplain who'd already put an arm around a young wife earlier that day and told her that her husband didn't make it. He fully expected to do the same with Brenda.

Pam Behnke, Brenda's best friend, also arrived to lend support. As head of the heart unit at the hospital, she knew the chest surgeons and had heard the paramedics' fears. She wanted to be there when the chaplain broke the news.

I don't remember much from those first moments in the emergency room. My most vivid memory is staring into the bright lights of the emergency room ceiling when suddenly the stricken face of my dear friend Dave Johnson poked into view. He was so scared. He's such a man's man, and I'd never seen him like that. I remember Brenda hovering so tenderly over me, but there was terror in her eyes. Pam stood by, of course. One of my pastors, Ray Henderson, came to my bedside. Everyone was so frightened.

But the moorings held fast. The Lord had heard my prayer, and there would be no surgery. A severe blow to the chest can cause a temporary, severe drop in blood pressure and traumatic shock, but in my case, there was no internal bleeding. Two hours later, I walked out of the hospital under my own power and far stronger for the experience and everything I learned from it.

What was I taught that day? Well, I learned that desperation is a native language in heaven. Yes, He understands every language—English, Spanish, Afrikaans, Chinese—but when it comes to His children, He is *very* fluent in Desperation and quick to hear our cry.

I also learned His grace absolutely covers *all* our sins, just like the Bible says. I didn't feel a trace of shame as I approached the Lord, and the fact that I was still engaged in the last skirmishes of my battle for purity wasn't an issue with Him. He'd already *won* the battle for my soul at Calvary, and that was the only one that counted for salvation. Eternal peace was mine.

Except for one thing.

The bald reality of suddenly sensing all that He'd done for me was staggering and astonishing in ways I hadn't felt before. Even now, when I think back on my desperation while slumped in my car, the tears well up in me. In the middle of that revelation, the depth of my love for Him was so real, so raw, and so overpowering that the desire to thank Him was indescribable. The overwhelming desire to have any small thing to lay at His feet in gratitude was amazing to me.

Sure, His grace frees us, but that doesn't diminish the importance of obedience. In fact, if anything, it increases it, because it is through obedience that we express our love for Him and gain those things to lay at His feet.

Obedience gives God room to maneuver in our lives. For me, my obedience in sexual purity gave me a testimony and something useful to say. In the end, it gave me nine books to lay at His feet the next time around.

The same has been true for Jasen. On the Tuesday before his wedding, I received a phone call from Channel Eleven in England, one of their national broadcast television stations. Because I am the author of *Every Man's Battle*, they were asking for a quote for their documentary on the growing chastity movement in their country.

"I can do better than that," I told the Brit. "My son is getting married Saturday, and he is about to kiss a woman for the first time—his bride. Are you interested?"

They were. They couldn't send a film crew that week, but one month later a Channel Eleven film crew interviewed Jasen and Rose. They spoke of the Lord's grace in their lives and the truths that backed their choices.

Obedience allows the Lord room to maneuver in your life. He can trust you with greater responsibilities. You don't have to chase ministry opportunities—they will chase you.

These are your last—and only—days on earth. How then should you live? The apostle Peter contemplated death and recorded his thoughts about this topic too. Through the inspiration of the Holy Spirit, Peter had this to say:

> What kind of people ought you to be? You ought to live holy and godly
> lives as you look forward to the day of God and speed its coming.... So
> then, dear friends, since you are looking forward to this, make every effort
> to be found spotless, blameless and at peace with him. (2 Peter 3:11–12, 14)

How then should you live? The Bible paints us a picture using the lives of thousands of pure men whose testimonies have already been written in the heavens:

> And they sang a new song before the throne and before the four living
> creatures and the elders. No one could learn the song except the 144,000
> who had been redeemed from the earth. These are those who did not defile
> themselves with women, for they kept themselves pure. They follow the
> Lamb wherever he goes. They were purchased from among men and
> offered as firstfruits to God and the Lamb. No lie was found in their
> mouths; they are blameless. (Revelation 14:3–5)

How then should you live? Live in a way that would qualify you for membership in the 144,000 Club. Could you currently qualify?

I didn't always live that way, but by God's grace, at least I can qualify now, and that's how we're supposed to use grace. Grace is not your get-out-of-jail-free card. Grace isn't your ticket to watch corrupt films or to enjoy lusty binges with your girlfriend. Grace is literally the power to live like a man in the midst of sensual chaos.

When I first read this passage from Revelation years ago, I figured those guys must have had some edge, some special dispensation from the Lord to live purely like that. Only recently did I notice this phrase: "for they kept themselves pure."

Did you hear that? *They kept themselves pure.* You don't need a special dispensation. You've already been given everything at salvation that you need in order to participate in the divine nature, and you can escape the corruption in the world caused by evil desires, just like these guys (2 Peter 1:3–4). You can protect the girls in your life. You've got what it takes already.

Don't waste His grace. Become something. Dream big.

Not long ago Michael rushed into my bedroom at two in the morning, his voice urgent and pleading. "Dad, Dad, I need to talk to you!"

I wasn't happy that he woke me up. Because of a book deadline, I'd written late into the evening and hit the sack at midnight, and I knew the alarm was set for 4 a.m. so I could catch an early flight in the morning.

Half asleep, I snapped, "Son, I'll call you in the morning between flights to talk about it. Just go to bed."

"No, Dad, please! I can't wait. I've got to talk to you right now. Please!"

I tossed the covers back and rolled up on the edge of the bed to look him in the eye. A familiar feeling—desperation—was etched all over his face. "Okay, Son, let's head to the family room. We can talk there."

After I sat down in my favorite chair, fourteen-year-old Michael poured out his heart about a deeply distressing and vivid dream with some heavy and disturbing shades of sensuality, speaking so fast and furiously that I could only catch every other word he said. He was terrified by that sensuality and terrorized by what it all meant to his future with God. To this day, I can't quite grasp why that deep fear and desperation had gripped him so tightly around the throat, but I did pick up enough to know it was the time to lay out the history of my family tree. He needed perspective. He needed hope.

I told him of the generational sin that had choked the joy out of my life as a young husband. I told him of looking into Jasen's two-year-old eyes and bursting into tears when I realized he was doomed to walk the same path I had. I told him of my Merle Hay Moment and my decision to fight for our name and our family tree, and I told him how Jasen joined me in this great destiny, opting out of the popularity game at school and standing up bravely for purity in high school and college. I told him every story I could think of about my battle, about Jasen, and about our new family destiny.

Finally, as the big hand of the clock swung its way past 3:30, I concluded this way: "Michael, once I'd won my battle for purity, there was finally one Stoeker living on this earth the way God called us to live sexually. Better yet, the Stoeker name no longer meant pornography, adultery, and divorce. Now it meant purity, fidelity, and holiness. And you know what? When Jasen stood up and grabbed the baton from my hand, there were two of us. If you join us, Michael, there will be three."

The desperation in Michael's face was gone, and something new had landed in its place.

"When you and Jasen grow up and get married," I continued, "perhaps you'll have a son, and maybe Jasen will have two. Once the both of you teach your boys the truth, there will be six Stoekers living like us. When they have *their* sons, perhaps there'll be twelve, and pretty soon there could be twenty-four Stoekers out there carrying our name well."

I paused. Michael's eyes had glazed over, mesmerized by the possibilities. Then, in a quiet, firm voice, he murmured, "I want that, Dad. I want that!"

That was one indelible moment, and I'll never forget that determined look in his eyes as his mind and spirit stepped up to his family destiny.

What about you, my friend? What do you want?

I hope to see that same look in your eye if we ever meet on this side of heaven. I believe you're ready to be a hero.

ACKNOWLEDGMENTS

From Jasen:

I would like to acknowledge those individuals who've had a strong influence upon the way I've lived. Without them, my wedding would have been less triumphant and my life would have more regrets. In short, this book would not exist.

I first want to thank my parents, Fred and Brenda, for the wonderful example they have been in my life. Dad and Mom, you tirelessly worked to raise me well, to discipline me when I was wrong and to train me in the ways I should go. I will be forever grateful for all that you taught me. You did a better job than any other parents I know.

I also want to thank my whole extended family for being great role models, but most especially my Grandma Gwen. She had an incredible faith and prayed tirelessly and is still one of the best examples of the Christian life I've ever seen.

Thanks to all my friends who contributed to this journey, including Dave and Amy Roe, who were an inspiration to me and served as a model for how a godly young couple should live, both before and after marriage. Thanks also to my dorm friend and summer roommate Austin Kelling, who began dating his bride about three months before I began dating Rose and provided a great, close-up example of what Christian dating should look like. He was a constant source of encouragement and accountability.

Thanks also to those authors who write about Christian dating and courtship, who help young guys like me to navigate the many obstacles that this culture puts between us and pure dating. Thanks to Jeramy Clark for his valuable perspectives on dating, and special thanks to Josh Harris for his fabulous book *Boy Meets Girl*. Rose and I read that book early in our relationship and found it extremely helpful.

And speaking of Rose, I'd also like to thank those who were great examples in *her* life, because they helped God provide the wonderful Christian girl who completed this story. Thanks to Pastor Dave, Angel, Seth, Debi, Steve, and all the others from Heartland. Your impact upon her, and us, has been more than you know. I send a huge, extra special thanks to David and Joy Gibson for raising such a wonderful, godly daughter. Where would we be without you two and all your years of commitment to each other and to raising Rose well? A guy couldn't ask for a better pair of in-laws!

Most importantly, thanks to my Savior, Jesus Christ. Without Your example, I would have no direction, and without Your sacrifice, I would have no life. Thank You, Lord!

NOTES

Introduction

1. Stephen Arterburn and Fred Stoeker, *Every Man's Battle* (Colorado Springs, CO: WaterBrook, 2000), 97.

Chapter 2

1. John Leland, "The Stories You Hid from Mom," *New York Times,* December 28, 2006.
2. David Shaw, "After 50 Years of Playboy, We All Live in Hef's World," *Los Angeles Times,* May 4, 2003.

Chapter 3

1. John Eldredge, *Wild at Heart: Discovering the Secret of a Man's Soul* (Nashville: Thomas Nelson, 2001), 9.

Chapter 4

1. "Billie Jean King's Text Inspired Sharapova," Associated Press (accessed at http://nbcsports.msnbc.com/id/22856899/site/21683474/).

Chapter 5

1. Simon Baron-Cohen, *The Essential Difference: Male and Female Brains and the Truth About Autism* (New York: Basic Books, 2003), 32–33, 36–37, 41, 45.
2. Stephen Arterburn and Fred Stoeker, *Every Man's Battle*, 135.

Chapter 7

1. Miriam Grossman, *Unprotected* (New York: Sentinel, 2006), 3–4.

2. Robert E. Rector, Kirk A. Johnson, and Lauren R. Noyes, "Sexually Active Teenagers Are More Likely to Be Depressed and to Attempt Suicide," Heritage Center for Data Analysis, 2003, www.heritage.org.

3. Kara Joyner and J. Richard Udry, "You Don't Bring Me Anything But Down: Adolescent Romance and Depression," *Journal of Health and Social Behavior,* 41 (December 2000): 369–91.

4. Grossman, *Unprotected,* 4–5.

5. Simon Baron-Cohen, *The Essential Difference: Male and Female Brains and the Truth About Autism* (New York: Basic Books, 2003), 21, 23, 32, 44–45.

6. Grossman, *Unprotected,* 4–5.

Chapter 8

1. John Eldredge, *Wild at Heart: Discovering the Secrets of a Man's Soul* (Nashville: Thomas Nelson, 2001), 8.

Chapter 15

1. Alex Harris and Brett Harris, *Do Hard Things* (Colorado Springs: Multnomah, 2008), 110–11.

Chapter 16

1. John Eldredge, *Wild at Heart: Discovering the Secret of a Man's Soul* (Nashville: Thomas Nelson, Inc., 2001), 140, 145.

2. Alex Harris and Brett Harris, *Do Hard Things* (Colorado Springs: Multnomah, 2008), 170–71.

How can any young man remain pure in the real world of sexual temptation?

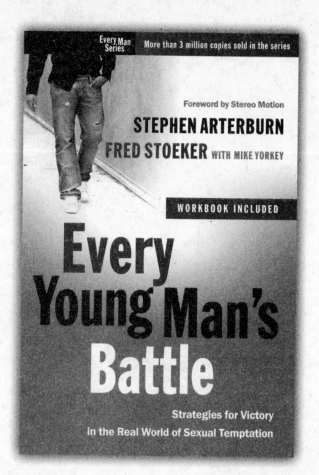

In this world guys are surrounded by sexual images that open the door to temptation. They're everywhere—on TV, billboards, magazines, music, the internet—and so easy to access that it sometimes feels impossible to escape their clutches. *Every Young Man's Battle* will show you how to train your eyes and your mind, how to clean up your thought life, and how to develop a realistic battle plan for remaining pure in today's sexually soaked culture.

WATERBROOK PRESS
www.waterbrookpress.com

A game-plan for staying sexually pure.

God sets a pretty high standard for sexual purity for his men: "Among you there must not be even a hint of sexual immorality" (Ephesians 5:3). Can you reach that standard? You've tried—and often succeeded. But if you haven't quite finished the job, you still need the right game day tactics to defeat temptation—and be God's champion. In *Tactics*, you can grab hold of these practical steps to deeper spiritual intimacy.

Trade hope and healing for your brokenness

ABOUT AVENUE MINISTRIES

An inter-denominational non-profit ministry founded by Clay and Susan Allen, AVENUE exists to offer healing to men caught in the snare of sexual compromise, and to wives devastated by betrayal.

To locate an AVENUE chapter in your area, or to begin one at your chuch, call 877.326.7000 or visit the website at www.AvenueResource.com.

ABOUT LIVING TRUE MINISTRIES

Under Fred and Brenda Stoeker's leadership, Living True Ministries operates on:

VISION:
To become a pivotal voice of reason in the midst of cultural decay.

MISSION:
To practically elucidate God's truth, encouraging and equipping men and women to rise up and be Christian, rather than to seem Christian.

VALUES:
Integrity, Congruency, Character, Urgency, and Normality.

If you are interested in a live appearance by Fred Stoeker, or for additional information, please email fred@fredstoeker.com or visit www.FredStoeker.com or www.BrendaStoeker.com.

Purity, reinforced through the Power of Music!

FRED STOEKER partners with **CHUCK DENNIE** and **CROWN ENTERTAINMENT** to create and release the music CD, *"WIN THIS WAR"*, a musical journey from sexual failure, to healing to true love. A great gift for sons, grandsons or any man longing for the purity God desires for his life.

Vocalists

Song List

1. THE LIE ~ Matthew West (3:53)
(from the album Happy, Matthew West)

2. REST WELL ~ Lee Spoken (3:33)
(from the album Drawn In, Lee Spoken)

3. FLOWERS BLOOM ~ Lee Spoken (4:31)
(from the album Drawn In, Lee Spoken)

4. GROWN MAN ~ downhere (5:08)
(previously unreleased)

5. CHANGE ~ Chuck Dennie and By the Tree (3:13)
(from the album These Days, By the Tree)

6. WIN THIS WAR ~ Chuck Dennie (3:10)
(previously unreleased)

7. GOD OF ALL MERCY ~ Michael O'Brien (3:59)
(new version of a song from Healing in Your Wings, Vineyard Music)

8. LET YOUR HEALING COME ~ Chuck Dennie (4:12)
(new version of a song from Offering of Love, Vineyard Music)

9. DESTINY ~ Chuck Dennie (4:18)
(previously unreleased)

10. LOVE OF CHRIST ~ Aaron Blanton (3:42)
(previously unreleased)

11. MIRACLE OF YOU ~ Michael O'Brien (3:32)
(new version of a song from All About Love, Steven Curtis Chapman)

12. WHEN LOVE TAKES YOU IN ~ Mike Weaver (4:34)
(new version of a song from All About Love, Steven Curtis Chapman)

www.WinThisWarCD.com

FOR BULK ORDERS CALL 1-800-661-9467